The Waldorf School and Threefold Structure

The Embarrassing Mandate

The Risk of Being an Anthroposophical Institution

by

Dieter Brüll

Published by:
 The Association of Waldorf Schools of North America
 3911 Bannister Road
 Fair Oaks, CA 95628

The Waldorf School and Threefold Structure
The Embarrassing Mandate
The Risk of Being an Anthroposophical Institution

© 1997 by AWSNA

ISBN # 1-888365-05-6

Originally published by Lazarus Press printed with the permission of Sigrid Mord-Brüll, his daughter.

Translated from the German by Thomas Forman & Trauger Groh

Editor and designer: David Mitchell

Proofreader: Nancy Jane

Curriculum Series

The Publications Committee of AWSNA is pleased to bring forward this publication as part of its *Curriculum Series*. The thoughts and ideas represented herein are solely those of the author and do not necessarily represent any implied criteria set by A.W.S.N.A. It is our intention to stimulate as much writing and thinking as possible about our curriculum, including diverse views. Please contact us with feedback on this publication as well as requests for future work.

David S. Mitchell
For the Publications Committee
A.W.S.N.A.

TABLE OF CONTENTS

Introductory Comments 4

Author's Foreword 7

The Basics of a School along Threefold Lines 11

Republican and Democratic 41

The Legal Committee 54

The Spiritual Organ 58

The Waldorf School and Waldorf Parents 63

The Waldorf School and State Funding 76

An Alternative Threefold Structure 81

A School with Two Classes of Faculty? 83

Appendix A 86

Appendix B 87

AWSNA Publications

impulses. Those who know the history of the Waldorf school also know that it was a child of the Threefold Movement. When the latter failed, Rudolf Steiner looked on the Waldorf school as the germ for the future rebirth of this movement. According to Steiner, pupils who leave the Waldorf school should master the principles of the threefold order like they've mastered the four basic arithmetical functions. In the course of my consulting activities, I encountered veritable fear and unwillingness at the word threefoldness. Everything that goes beyond theory, everything pointing to the need to intervene with the given, primarily structural relationships is met with distrust, or even with hostility. Without knowing what a threefold school structure looks like, the argument arises that the co-workers are not mature enough for it, and/or that the introduction of such a structure involves an unjustifiable risk. Indeed, this is the risk of being an anthroposophical institution! By the way, this statement does not apply only to the schools but to the entire institutional anthroposophical life, with certain exceptions. Here the Waldorf school has merely the right of the firstborn, because it was the first institution with which the anthroposophical movement went public. But today I know of more therapeutic institutions than schools, at least in the Netherlands, who strive for the threefold order.

In no way should the individual institutions be reproached with this lack of examples, this hostility against the social impulse. Each one has the right to form along the wishes of its co-workers or its leaders. Yet none have the right to call the results of the process – a copy of our present societal structure – the threefold order. Yet exactly this is the common trend. Psychologically, this is very understandable, because one finds oneself in the painful position of not wanting to accept or reject Steiner's concept that the Waldorf schools should pioneer the future threefold order. Furthermore, one should know that the manner in which a school forms itself has significance beyond that school. A school with a structure not conforming to the threefold principle harms all of humanity, because the latter is robbed of the opportunity to orient itself on a model that is practically functional and appropriate to the consciousness of today. Those who wring their hands about the monstrosities of our times, and ask what we could do, would find the answer by starting threefoldness on the very spot where destiny has placed them!

Distancing ourselves from the threefold order also does damage to the anthroposophical life. Manfred Schmidt Brabant in his role as section leader presented the following schematic of the structure of the social-scientific section during a public meeting dedicated to its renewal:

"The achievements, which flow from the General Section into the different sections where they lead to spiritual scientific deepening of specific areas, have their foundation in the social-scientific section." This is how the different sections begin to grow roots in society. We think about Rudolf Steiner's words: "spirit without form performs no deeds." It is the task of the social impulse to create the form. By means of this form the remaining anthroposophical impulses are able to incarnate in the life of society at large. Yet, if the institutions which want to transmit the anthroposophical impulses are not anthroposophical *institutions*, i.e. are not structurally based on the anthroposophical social impulse, then the entire edifice of the free school is floating in thin air.

Because of their history and of their social mission, the schools are, in the first place, called upon to take up this social impulse. This book is intended as a contribution toward this task. If one does not come to terms with this task, a tendency already surfacing today will prevail. The school movement will break up into small theocratically directed sectarian schools on one hand, and on the other, into schools which lose their identity by conforming to the demands of the unlawful prince of this world. Without always clearly recognizing the cause for it, this identity crisis is already being experienced in many quarters in our day. Yet many may be awakened by the pain over what is being lost in this process. This is the ray of hope in defeat.

AWSNA Publications

Experience and practical indications will, in my opinion, do more to further this awakening than philosophical observations, for the latter remain edifying literature if they lack practical experience. Those who look for the background of the following chapters will find it in my *Anthroposophical Social Impulse,* (Schaffhausen, 1984). There one can find the basis of Rudolf Steiner's work. With a few exceptions I have omitted this foundation. I also omitted comparisons with other publications on the same subject. The interested reader will find his or her way. Additionally, I refer to the references at the end of the book.

Appendix B, "A Micro-Social Dissertation", goes beyond the framework of this book. Here an attempt is made to show something of the intrinsic, that is – the individual social impulse – which is a moral issue. Therefore, it must neither be demanded nor expected. The only thing that can be shown is the framework, in fact the threefold structure within which the impulse can be made available to an individual who wants it. This can make it clear that what is here presented in reference to the Waldorf schools really applies to *every* school. The social impulse, the social gesture, would have no validity if it were limited to institutional Anthroposophy. The social impulse is a human one and hence, by its very nature, Christian. Many misunderstandings are growing up around the concept "social" and around the task of learning what is social. I did not consider it to be superfluous to include this untimely observation of the social issue in a book dealing with the threefold social structure in practical school life, because most of what is being sold under the name of "social" is nothing but refined egoism.

It only remains for me to express my happy thanks to the friends who came to the help of my feeble German and of my amateurish knowledge of German conditions. I am also thankful to the free publishing house "Lazarus" and the threefold publishing house "Nearchus" who have made the publication of this book possible. Lastly, I owe thanks to the Waldorf schools. I hope that I can repay a debt I owe them for all the education and knowledge they have given me with these thoughts.

Chapter I

Basics of a School along Threefold Lines

One can, of course, simply start a new school with a handful of children, parents with great expectations, and one or two teachers. In the absence of constraining legislation, it is even quite legal to do this. In a little while one discovers that one has created a structure without intent to do so. Yes, but whether this structure is really appropriate, would be comparable to getting a dress that really fits at a church bazaar. One can obtain a model from the government or from the national Waldorf school association. The state follows a definite pattern when it founds a school. I guarantee that one will get used to it, just as British children became used to going to school in a uniform and would not have it any other way. One rarely considers that the way a school is structured really determines its entire lifestyle. Once one has discovered this unpleasant fact, there may be something to be said for planning ahead of time and for considering the basic structure required by Waldorf schools. Let us give this a try!

We must impose two restrictions on ourselves as we embark on this work. The first one is to strictly exclude any thoughts, even secondary ones, about the legality of what we wish to do. Once we know specifically what we want, it will be easy to find a lawyer who can translate this into something that bears the "stamp of approval." Anybody who wants to get anywhere proceeds in this manner anyway. The second restriction prohibits any question regarding economic feasibility. A bean counter can be found later on. Now what have we done? For shame, we have created structure. We have made a rule for ourselves. Let's phrase it positively: we have created the boundary within which we can work freely. As we look back, we shall discover that these simple rules have touched on principles that will stay with us on our journey of discovery.

Taken by themselves these considerations would not really require rules. It would merely be more difficult to obtain the desired result without a structure. Informal thinking requires no structure. This may well be the reason why thinkers often dislike creating structured systems. I was told that in Vienna there existed a school association without a school. And this existed for ten years! Here one could fantasize to one's heart content, because what came out never had any consequence. One could think as hard as one wanted about the question whether the final exam was to be internal or external to the school. As long as there was not even a kindergarten, all this remained up in the air. This informality – albeit as structure – will resurface later in our considerations as a positive principle.

The moment any activity is started, it needs to be structured. I am aware of the fact that many people think that the structure should grow out of the work. Unfortunately, this is wrong. What should grow out of the work is *substance*. The work itself, rather than rules and dogma, should create substance. But a structure has to be in place no later than the day the school opens its doors. Whoever steps over the threshold has to know that now the rules of the school are in place. What would the teachers say if a neighbor would appear and noisily insist on being heard, as is the custom among neighbors? Or if a mother would show up in a classroom and distribute ordinary oil colors among the little ones instead of the "silly" water colors? "I understand, here; rules exist for others. But does a decent person like me need them?" We shall encounter this problem again later. For now let us pin down that the first organizing action consists in the creation of an inside and an outside. The school acquires a skin. It may at first be too thin; it may get too thick. Whatever its character, it is an absolute must for a social organism, just like for the human one. There is no life without this skin. "Formless spirit cannot act," said Rudolf Steiner.

The mission of the school is the second element of its structural organization. Formulating a mission statement very early on is a necessity. Every institution takes its place within society as an organism with a mission, which one resolves to fulfill. One may create a club, a foundation, a cooperative, or a civil rights organization. In every case one will have to declare its objective. Society has a right to know what ensouls this new organization, this new citizen of the earth. This objective has to be made public and accessible to everybody. A Waldorf school will have to state in some way that its objective is pedagogy according to Rudolf Steiner.

Setting this objective has far reaching consequences. In part these belong to the sphere of rights. Actions of the institution that do not pertain to the mission statement are void. The fact that this objective setting focuses the entire life of the organization on the objective is far more important. As we shall see, this can be regarded as a concentration of its forces but it has far reaching limitations as well.

A school is an organism. An organism forms organs to carry out specific functions within the institution. These organs do not come about of themselves. They are put in place by people and can only work as intended, if people use them in a functional manner. Waldorf schools are founded on self-government. Here a social organism is viable within a wide margin. Desirable organs may be absent, and the presence of redundant or noxious ones (tumors) need not destroy the institution. This allows liberties and, thus, presents certain dangers as well. Let us first define the vital organs.

In every social organism there exists spiritual life, the life of rights, and the economic sphere. Because the institution has an objective, it has, by definition, an economic life. This latter life encompasses the economic/purposeful cooperation toward a given objective. Yet the co-workers must find some way to come to terms with each other and with the outer world, that which is outside the boundaries of the institution. This is where the sphere of rights lives. And, finally, each co-worker wants to realize her or his self, otherwise they would become automatons. This self-realization represents the flowering of the spiritual life of the institution. We should not interpret this as an egocentric act, rather as that which a person creates as his or her own pedagogical impulse. The emphasis has shifted in the course of the centuries. In our time we are positioned at the leading edge of our personalities, and when we live in harmony with our times, we have fully withdrawn our "I" being from the institution. We want to work on it, as it were, from the outside, so that it promotes our inner life as much as possible. We introduce our "I" or ego impulses into the institution with every member of our soul. Thus, these spheres represent the content of the institution, the real reason for its existence. The fact that we also bring along what is unpurified in our soul leads to social problems. These necessitate a very thorough structure.

Rudolf Steiner discovered the threefold social order as the structural principle for the social organism of our times. In accordance with this principle every person participates in the spiritual life, the rights life, and the economic life in three fully autonomous spheres. Only the outline of the structure is given. The structure itself, i.e. the content, is being determined by the human beings living within the organism. Within the life of an institution such radical threefold division is impossible due to the very existence of the objective. If the social organism is in accord with its time, it has no objective. Every objective suppresses its subjects. They turn into pawns of the striving to reach it. If the objective falls by the wayside, the three spheres can be autonomous in the truest sense – in this case the well being of the totality of the organism can fully depend on their voluntary cooperation. On the other hand, if institutions have a mission, this implies that people's personal development must be constrained – our freedom is being affected. One could call this a "fall of man." We are forced to work together, because we are no longer hunters or collectors. Cooperation is no longer subject to our free volition. We have to sacrifice our (total) independence. This "fall of man" leads us into becoming social beings just as the biblical fall had led us into individualization. (No argument against institutional threefoldness has impressed me as little as the one which states that Steiner has [almost] never said anything about it. He said nothing about AIDS either, yet nobody is likely to object that anthroposophical doctors treat this disease. In fact, Steiner has shed so much light on the human organism that one can use the knowledge to break new ground. It is also true that he said enough about the social organism to make it possible to "attack" institutions with this knowledge. If threefoldness is derived from what is human, as Steiner says, then why should one not consider it when building institutions? Is it not true that humans place their whole being into these? Whether one calls this threefold social life, or whether one reserves this term for the macro-sphere is a question of semantics and not of concepts.)

This should, however, not stop us from minimizing the constraints of freedom as much as possible. Each one of the three areas can guarantee that every co-worker maintains the respect of his personality, even though life (within the school) takes place within the framework of the objective, and even though, for economic reasons, it must fit into the overall striving toward the objective and has to conform to majority decisions. Freedom is constrained in all three areas. Three organs are created to form, as it were, a shell and, thus, structure what the co-worker brings to the school as his very own impulses. Let us consider these three organs.

The Organ of Spiritual Life

What we have to deal with here is the central organ of every institution that sees its principal task within the life of the spirit. Most Waldorf schools have this organ, most frequently under the name of the College of Teachers. I prefer not to use this name. All too often elements not belonging to it creep into this meeting. These may confuse the reader.

The only thing that should take place within this organ is exclusively spiritual life. Except for activities expressly reserved for other realms, the spiritual life permeates the entire school. Within our context it is imperative that it is based in its purest form, i.e. on the life of the spirit only. Every member of the organ must have the opportunity to express *every* point of view related to the spiritual life, even if it is controversial. Here it is not even necessary to conform to the principles of the bylaws. These command only the actions, not the ideas. Mr. Strangelove is free to suggest that one deals with nervous and irritating pupil behavior by administering a daily dose of valium. This will raise a thunderstorm, but it does no harm. Mr. Strangelove does not exceed the rules. This is done by Mr. Wiseguy who suggests not to waste time on such "rubbish" because forced medications are prohibited anyway. Mr. Wiseguy will have to come up with an argument from the spiritual sphere, not from the sphere of rights.

This freedom has its price. A statement within this organ must not be binding by itself, nor taken together with similar statements from other co-workers. Indeed, it does not even commit the person who makes it. One can concur with his view, one can even try to convince others, but one must not tie anybody down. Socially, this view has the character of a suggestion. Each individual is free to deal with it the way he or she wants to. Nothing is being voted on here; neither is a decision made under the guise of a consensus.

Let's take the practical example that a pupil conference had unanimously concluded that it would be wrong for Oscar's development to ignore his fresh behavior. In a given class situation it is still up to his teacher to ignore the epithet "idiot" clearly directed at him. Does one really wish to make the teacher act against his pedagogical conviction? This is not appropriate, even if this conviction differs from what was said in the conference room when Oscar was discussed. We shall come across quite different reasons, but just from this point of view, it should not even occur to anyone that it would be appropriate to " make this or that clear to our colleague."

We used a purely pedagogical case, one fully within the realm of the spiritual life. Yet there are many problems that occur in a school where the spiritual aspect is only part of the picture. The classrooms have to be painted, a question of the economic life (a need) and of the rights life (making money available). But, since colors have a pedagogical significance in Waldorf schools, the organ of the spiritual life may also want to have a say. "Last time the yellow was too lemony; perhaps this time care could be taken to make it warmer." Mrs. Peculiar has asked for leave of absence for good reason. This is a juridical question because she wants to be absolved from her responsibilities. Yet the situation in her class – e.g. certain tensions – makes this appear problematical.

Thus, the spiritual organ has a right to demand that the spiritual aspect of every problem be subjected to its judgment. In practice one can imagine that all suggested decisions are available for review. *Everybody* then has the right to ask for discussion within the spiritual organ. *But,* no one has the right to include the aspect of the rights life and the economic aspects in their considerations. No matter who it may be, if he or she ignores this constraint, they must inexorably be silenced.

To consider the entire reach of each one of the three aspects separately is primarily a question of social hygiene. And beyond this it is a practical aid against the endless and therefore, tiring discussions that jump from one track to another. For instance, during a debate, in the spiritual organ, about the plan for a new auditorium, Mr. Sourpuss must be interrupted with a bone jarring bang of the gavel when he interjects, "But we cannot pay for this!" This is true, even when the colleagues have roamed around in non-affordable wishes.

Mr. Sourpuss should reserve his concerns for the economic organ. When one speaks of abandoning the exit exam, one can bet that Mr. Wiseguy will unburden himself with the discovery that a Waldorf school is not allowed to do this. Again, the gavel will drop, "Please stick to the rules of this organ; you can speak about the rules of the authorities within the rights organ!" Institutions within the spiritual life, such as schools, have the very task to discuss the desirability of what comes out of the spiritual impulse with the utmost clarity. To translate this to reality will then need the help of the two other spheres or even external expertise.

Difficulties are unavoidable. The participants learn only gradually to differentiate among the three areas. In seminars and training sessions I have sometimes arranged the acting out a social drama around a problem case in the life of an institution from its structural aspect. What struck me was that even some participants who had largely absorbed threefoldness got into trouble when faced with a practical case. Therefore, one needs guidance until one has lost one's uncertainty (and to prevent wrongheaded ideas from sneaking in). An impartial moderator is needed, if nobody among the co-workers has a feel for threefoldness right down to their fingertips. This person has to bang the gavel as soon as anybody crosses the boundaries of the organ. To begin with, an outsider has an additional advantage. It is easier for him to interrupt senior people. Sooner or later all the colleagues get used to the procedure!

It goes without saying that such an outside mediator does not participate in the conversation. He or she merely controls the procedure. Later, the task is taken over by the discussion leader or by one of the participants. The moderator must also guard against the restriction of freedom through the words: "If this happens, I leave the school!" At least in the area of the spiritual life, such blackmail is inappropriate. It blocks the free flowing of various points of view.

Who belongs by right to the organ of spiritual life? It is easy to define this: it is every co-worker who looks at his task as being pedagogical. (Not how others see his task!) It does not hurt to have someone sit in whose right to be there can be doubtful, because here no decisions are being made. For example, this might be a teacher whose only task is to drill the candidates for an exam in a particular subject. Such a person will hardly be interested in participating in the meetings. Yet perhaps he wants to enrich his didactic task with a pedagogical element? And again, why should one limit participation to teachers? Are they really the only pedagogues working in the school? Perhaps you noticed that I did not speak of teachers but about co-workers. I did it for this very reason. In my children's school there was a janitor whose pedagogical qualities exceeded those of most of the teachers. If they could not deal with a pupil, he or she was sent to this man. He managed the most notorious characters quite easily. How much his participation could have enriched the discussions of pupils! By what arrogance did one rob oneself of this opportunity?

In addition to those who are immediately involved with the children, one can invite experts to specific meetings. This is of special importance in case certain subjects are not strongly represented within the school. Somewhere one must be able to find a specialist on puberty and somewhere else one on the subject of punishment, etc. This practice represents the essence of the style of work within a truly free spiritual life. In the search for truth there may be a quarrel between different philosophies, even when economic interests have been excluded. Yet the fact of working together on *one* pedagogical task may develop the tendency of looking for the person with the best qualifications. Call this an inverted hierarchy, or perhaps aristocracy, in view of the mastery of this or that person to deal with his area of work. It may also be called anarchy, because nobody is forced to accept anything from anyone else. In any case, a guest adds nothing new to the situation. By its own nature the life of the spirit is of an advisory nature.

But the parents and the pupils most certainly do not belong in the organ of the spiritual life. The parents are excluded due to their ultimate responsibility in their own sphere of education (see chapter 5 – Waldorf School and Waldorf Parents), which in no way needs to be influenced by that of the teachers. The children do not belong, because they are the object of the pedagogical effort.

I have stated radically that our conference does not make a single decision. I must name the one exception which confirms the rule. The College of Teachers chooses its chairperson. If this person would be prescribed from any other source, the autonomy of the College would be lost. Is the organ of the spiritual life then forbidden to appoint subcommittees to work on specific themes? This may vary. If it is a question of co-workers freely working together, nothing needs to be decided. The fact that such a subcommittee exists may result in tacitly leaving the subject up to them. However, if the conference wants to obtain a study of a specific subject (possibly within a certain schedule), then a committee, responsible to the conference, is needed. The conference, however, will have to leave it to the juridical organ to assign responsibility, because it has no authority to make anyone responsible. Of course, it has the right to suggest to the juridical organ the people who would best serve on such a committee. And it is also understood that the juridical organ will accept the suggestion, unless very exceptional conditions prevail. This may appear to be a redundant formality. This is not the case, and we shall encounter this principle again.

The Economic Organ

Let us now jump to the organ which represents the polar opposite. In contrast to the life of the spirit, which affords the co-worker the greatest opportunity to unfold, the economic organ, representing the economic life of the school, has the exclusive function of providing services.

To start off with, let us once and for all do away with the idea that this is where the finances are being managed. To be sure, money is involved in providing goods and services in a school as everywhere else. But money is involved in *all* social events, in the pop concert just as much as in the Anthroposophical Society's branch meeting. In the final analysis any citizen's legal affairs are resolved in the award of monetary damages, because even today's judge has no physical powers to coerce. Money casts the shadow wherein all our deeds and omissions become materially tangible. Of course, there are many critical areas in the flow of money. The most important ones for the school are the establishment of tuition and the decision how to use the money. Both are juridical matters. The economic organ's primary functions are different.

Managing the economy means to satisfy needs. It does not involve consumption as such, but the path taken by what is needed until it is available to the person in need. This requires two things, to know the nature of the need *and* the objective, namely to bring product into the hands of the consumer in the most economic, i.e. efficient, manner. The economic organ has to do justice to both tasks. They are fundamentally different.

Let us first consider the second one. In order to reach the objective in the most efficient manner, one needs to know it. The organ can only work insofar as the objective has been defined, at least hypothetically. To say "We have so much money, what shall we do with it?" is just as misleading for the economic organ as "We have no money therefore, we cannot do anything." One can study how to increase income or decrease expenses. It is not one's task to make any decisions in this respect. Once we are well aware of this, we can allow Mr. Sourpuss his sway. He can figure out what the desired auditorium will cost, how much one saves by not roofing it over, what the extra costs with the lazuring way of painting will be, etc. The more definition exists, the easier it is to calculate, and the less leeway exists for alternative suggestions. Additionally, the planners will do better not to speculate. They present calculations which show that percentages could be earned if one were to use a standardized block journal. They are not even allowed to be amazed that a number of teachers are beside themselves about this interference with their freedom as teachers. They get involved with the complicated question of how many pupils (and tuition fees) would be lost, if the exit exam were to be abolished. They can even introduce the variable that, in this case, all government support would be withdrawn (without researching this question, which is a legal one). They should not be prejudiced by the fact that the parents want to have the exit exam. Here one can work objectively, because the calculations are used only for information. This is true, too, for suggestions to streamline the internal organization. A decision is not made here any more than in the organ of the spiritual life. This type of work clearly shows that much experience is needed, and the efforts of many specialists will be involved. Committees for these purposes are best created out of a free impulse without official interference. The challenge is: where can I help with my knowledge and experience?

We enter a far more touchy realm with the other tasks of the economic organ. If one wants to satisfy needs, one has to know them. The arrogance of the life of the spirit presents an obstacle here. There one thinks one knows what people need. And, should practical life prove the opposite, so much the worse for practical life. "Those folk don't know themselves what they really want." ("But of course I know it."). But if the parents' complaints have even found an advocate in a teacher, then an outburst on the part of the great spirits occurs: "If the parents don't like it, let them look for another school!" This says the right thing in the wrong way.

It would certainly be wrong to consider a school only as an enterprise where the producers (the teachers) sell their goods (pedagogy) to the pupils (parents). Yet this aspect applies also to Waldorf schools. However, within the framework of the economy, the question is whether a merchandise is good for the buyer and not whether it is justified. The question can merely be: is there a need? By the way, this does not oblige me to produce an answer for every need. Let's look at an example.

A mother gets up and asks whether the eurythmy lessons should be discontinued and replaced with ballet lessons. Well, what happens if the same great spirit says to the lady in deepest chest tones of shock, whether she knows that she has sent her child to a Waldorf school? Or if his colleague carries on about the physical and soul damage caused by ballet? Perhaps that mother would retreat in the face of such massive power, but only to gather other mothers around herself outside the hall to form a complaining club aimed at the arrogant, sectarian teachers in their ivory tower. And how many parents will not want to be heard, because they are afraid to say the wrong thing as a result of this debacle? Our three teachers are better off if they arrange a lecture about Anthroposophy and ballet. In this way they stay within the sphere of the life of the spirit. Everyone interested in the subject can attend.

Within the economic life one must assume that *every* need, and therefore every satisfaction, is legitimate. In all honesty one can agree with the mother who wants to see her need filled like anyone else's. Once a wish is registered there is no saying "no." With this as a ground rule, one no longer feels pressured or, worse, ridiculed, as a consumer. In this case one also accepts that the school adds: "only we unfortunately don't sell this product, namely ballet lessons. We have no teachers for this and cannot hire any, because it does not fit our overall teaching philosophy. We simply have a particular set objective, just like other schools have different ones. In the same way there are clothing stores with various styles of dress, so that everyone can find his own store, according to his or her tastes. May we perhaps help you find a school where ballet is in the curriculum?" Or in the worst case: "Why don't you start your own school along with those who have the same wish?"

One can, of course, show one's principled side vis-à-vis the parents. This is doubtless a valid option. But to get to this level of response takes a process of many years. Yet, we are faced with the problem today and have to solve it today.

Today it can only be solved if one looks at it as an economic problem. This is the right question for most parents: who satisfies the pedagogical wishes we have for our children? And, just like in everyday life, one will have to compromise here, too. It makes no sense to be angry with my greengrocer, because he has only sprayed apples. *I* have to make a choice in this situation; do I drive for half an hour to the organic store, or do I swallow poison?

The above does not mean that one should get rid of the parents with empty phrases by moving the problems over to the economic life. On the contrary, one should seriously consider every registered need as to whether and how one could meet it. One should do this simply to be human. But it is almost obligatory in our time, when it is almost impossible to found one's own school, except in some protected, sheltered corner. The economic organ is not a packaging machine. It has the concrete function to act as counterweight to the self satisfaction over having a well established enterprise. Only too often the relationship to the parents is on the wrong track. (This cannot be camouflaged with a parent council.) This is usually due to fear, sometimes due to an unwillingness, to enter into conversation with these persons. This can escalate to the view that the school has everything to do with the pupils and nothing to do with the parents. This is founded on our pedagogical arrogance. It is surprising how quickly parental wishes are labeled as "unrealizable," whereas one conforms to the wishes of the state without questions. For example. the Waldorf schools in the Netherlands have fought tooth and nail against any say on the part of the parents. This went on for decades. When the state asked for parental councils, all but two Waldorf schools conformed.

The economic organ is the place for parents and other participants to register their wishes. In the same way let it be the place where the teachers go public with their concerns, such as lack of teachers, decreasing contributions, retrenchments of staff, controversy within the teaching staff, unpleasantness with the authorities, quarrels with the union, and whatever else one usually tends to sweep under the rug. Is it not true that we all have more understanding and are more willing to help if we know a person's problems than when all is presented as working smoothly and harmoniously, while rumors of messed up issues are already circulating? Does anybody believe that anything can remain hidden in a school?

Finally, there is the question of who should work in such an economic organ. As far as managing the economy is concerned, the participants should probably be primarily co-workers. The engagement of an outsider should be based on a decision of the rights organ. Apart from what has been said about the spiritual life organ, which applies here as well, one needs to take to heart that concrete suggestions often afford deep insights into the intimate facts of the life of a school. (However, in my view, institutions should have no intimate areas.) The personal areas of co-workers must be protected. And again these do not include what a co-worker has said or done as part of his function.)

When the economic organ becomes the ear of the school and wants to hear what needs come forward, the situation is quite different. Here everyone is welcome, if they think that it is desirable to have a Waldorf school in this place. This includes *all* teachers, probably most of the remaining co-workers, the parents, and prospective parents as well. It also includes other personalities who, for whatever reasons, are friends of the Waldorf school system: doctors, ministers, farmers, politicians, entrepreneurs, etc. Should somebody prove to be not only an occasional nuisance but a trouble maker as well, one can as a last instance ask the organ of the rights life to prohibit such a person from entering the school. In the end pupils too belong to the latter category. After, say the tenth grade the louts suddenly become ladies and gentlemen. Wherever one has experienced this, it was found, rather surprisingly, how well thought out, sober, and competent the contributions from that side turned out to be.

One more touchy subject: the parents council. I have only negative experiences with this body, in particular if it is somehow elected by the parent body or if it has been named to represent it in some roundabout manner. It is painful to have to say this, because it represents the investment of so much good will. The economic organ deals with concrete questions, not with ideologies, nor with partisanship. However, elected parent representatives will always tend to make judgments based on pleasing those who will (potentially) vote for them, instead of basing them on the matter on hand. If one cannot get around legislation prescribing a parent council, one should counter-act it by opening the door widely to all, as we have seen appropriate for the economic organ. This dilutes the *function*. No voting takes place within an economic organ. It is the place for evaluating questions.

I have covered the economic organ in detail, because it is terra nova for most schools. It is assumed that questions of rights are rigorously excluded from the previous organs when the above is followed by discussions of the rights organ. There we shall argue for a strictly democratic attitude. Great caution is needed in the economic area not to allow the state to force its own degenerated legal system on the school. This has catastrophic consequences, particularly in the economic organ.

Let me also point out that the economic life organ is functionally no stranger in the Waldorf schools. Something resembling it was built in from the very start as parent evenings. These do not exist to discuss pedagogical problems of the parents and their children. (This belongs to the house visitations, which represent the spiritual life in the micro-area of communication with the parents.) Least of all do they exist for educating the parents, a purpose for which the evenings have often been abused. In contrast to the organ of economic life, here – limited to the grade – parents should air their questions and teachers their concerns.

The Rights Organ

Individuals by themselves cannot order their activities in a threefold way. This is so, because she or he has no sphere of rights. We can form resolutions but no decisions. To decide what is right, a minimum of two persons are needed. On the other side of this coin, it is true that wherever two or more persons act together, a social situation arises.

This can be seen in a Waldorf School. Many people work together toward the objective. Additionally, there are external relationships in the sphere of rights vis-à-vis the parents, the authorities, the suppliers, etc. Wherever "me" or "you" comes in question, rights are involved. What is right involves the question of what it is I deserve in relation to others. The principle that human dignity is untouchable is the basis of our rights. Both written and unwritten rules are derived from this. They are not always correct, indeed, seldom so. Human right, *lex humana*, is susceptible to errors. It should, therefore, be in constant flow: how we can better do justice to human dignity.

One can always replace an old rule by a new one or abolish it altogether. This, however, applies only to a *future point in time.* Until then, the old rule prevails, even if everybody finds it to be absurd. "Misery knows no imperatives" is the common euphemism for one's own priorities.

This applies to what one has mutually decided upon. It does not, however, apply to the following:

a) to what a school as one party has agreed upon with another party. Contrary to frequently held views, even unanimous rights organ cannot unilaterally change a contract with a teacher, with parents, or with outsiders. I have experienced that the decision to have no school on Saturday was simply announced to the parents of a Waldorf school. When this was protested against, the reasons for it were suddenly pedagogical! The meeting of the College of Teachers was supposed to have autonomy over this. Here self-righteousness and lacking a sense of justice had a heyday.

b) the rule also does not apply where one has not been part of the decision. However strongly the state wants to convince us of the opposite, it follows that whether one should abide by laws placed on us by others is a pure question of opportunity and has nothing to do with morality. For example, catholic sociology still holds that one does not have to obey unjust laws. I have understanding for the situation where one bows to the power that forces unjust school legislation. I have equal understanding for schools that seek ways of circumventing unjust laws. And I have the deepest respect for those who out of conviction violate the regulation and accept the consequences. The (honest) student of history discovers that we have to thank those acting from conviction for *all* progress.

In a threefold school the decisions are made within the rights organ. This gives priority to the question as to who belongs to this organ . The answers to this are usually rather interesting. Is it important that one sticks to his decision? Well, it would be nice, but should we not assume that everyone does that already? And the school has no power against the repetitive sinner other than exclusion. The one who carries the school in his inner life? This criterion would violate human dignity. Indeed, only an examination of the soul life of another person could define conformity to such a condition. For shame! If we proceed along this route, we shall soon find that all is well only among the great ones in the spirit, thus reestablishing theocracy. It would hold fewer dangers to assign the power of decision to those who have joined an esoteric circle. Often this is the basis of membership of an internal conference (or of whatever name one gives to that organ). This means that there are people who reserve the right to determine whether a co-worker is capable of decisions and who place themselves on a higher moral level than other colleagues. Here we encounter a part of the tendency to classify the co-workers as well as parents (see chapter 8) into those who can carry responsibility and those who are incapable of this. If we just saw an echo of theocracy, here is one of the caste systems. All this no longer belongs to the age of the consciousness soul.

We shall have to find out who belongs in the rights organ from within that organ. We wind up carrying responsibility but in a different context, namely that only persons who will carry the consequences of their decisions are to do the deciding. The economic life of our time looks for every possible way to get rid of this rule for the very reason that it is a matter of justice that one has to accept the consequences of one's actions. An example is to give one's enterprise the official form of being incorporated or a stock corporation. The profits belong to the holder of bonds or stocks. When losses occur, they are transferred to the company, because somebody must carry the burden which the legally responsible person cannot pay – or should they? A threefold school should not copy this antisocial feature. In our context this means three things:

1. The co-workers should be working as free entrepreneurs, for example, as partners in a partnership. There may be exceptions to this, but the responsibility vis-à-vis the partnership is real only if one is subject to the consequences of one's deeds – if necessary all the way to personal bankruptcy. For now, I would like to overlook the fact that legal requirements often force the school to make co-workers employees. I will only remark that one can think of something similar, e.g. personal guarantees.

2. Partners receive no salary; instead they get a portion of the financial yield of the year. Not only does this provide the basis for separating work from income (more to this later), it also addresses the problem of making one's life really dependent on the well being of one's school, thus establishing an existential connection.

3. Co-workers are not members of the organ of the life of rights, if they are not existentially connected with the school, because they wish to have security and, therefore, a fixed salary, or because someone is only working part time or to an insignificant extent in the school. This applies to high

dignitaries as well! I want to stress the fact that there are many practical options, depending on conditions. The problem of the unwillingness to give immediate rights to make decisions to any green newcomer can also be solved in this sphere. It takes two to decide whether and when one accepts a newcomer as a partner. A trial period may make sense. During this time one receives a fixed income. Abuses by a small faction are prevented by the rule that after a predetermined time, e.g. two years, the applicant must either be admitted or dismissed.

The exclusive nature of the rights organ presents additional problems. It can happen that a decision regarding the interests of a co-worker who does not belong to the organ must be made. Nowadays this is more the rule than the exception, yet one should be conscious of the fact that it conflicts with another principle of justice, namely that every mature person has the right of a say in anything that concerns his rights. Hence, it will be well in this case to invite the co-worker to sit in and to give her or him every opportunity to defend her or his interests. Such a person, however, has no vote. As we shall see, there is a way of compensating for this.

Let us turn to what happens within the rights organ. First of all, there are a few, yet highly important, *pure* problems of justice which can be taken care of without the cooperation of the other two organs. An example would be remuneration. Then, secondly, there are problems where the life of rights is only a part, such as the acceptance of new co-workers and pupils. Thirdly, there is the bestowing of authorizations. This usually hovers between the other two areas. Although we cannot deal with these three areas in detail. we shall sketch them sufficiently to clarify the differences.

Remuneration should be a pure problem of justice. What should another person be given in relation to myself, to my colleagues, and to our students? Here I must explicitly warn again against remuneration according to need. One usually understands this as a situation where one assesses how much one needs and asks for this. Let us not deceive ourselves. Self assessment becomes the child of self over-assessment, a trait we all share. Is it reasonable that we expect that (all!) our co-workers have progressed to the point where they feel their colleagues' needs as strongly as their own? This not being the case, all sorts of pressure is used to make the co-worker in question estimate her or his needs to be as small as possible. Remuneration according to need turns out to be exploitation under the guise of ideology. On top of this, so as to avoid rebellion ("Why does he get so much and I so little?"), remuneration is treated as a state secret.

    I don't object against "living out of the same pot," i.e. to take what one needs out of the cash box without accounting for it to anyone. One must only be aware of the fact that this practice attempts to live in a way appropriate for the next cultural epoch. In a school this would work only if *no* co-worker is exploited by this practice. Otherwise, another two classes of co-workers are created again: those who belong to the brotherhood and the laymen. Exploitation always leads to the opposite of what is attempted. In this case: Mrs. Lovely's new shoes and Mr. Trendy's new car will create instant jealousy, low opinion for the co-worker who is enslaved by materialism and . . . increase in one's own needs.

    I call it fitting for our time if my income consists, of the amount which the other co-workers place at my disposal. This is how we can also read it in Rudolf Steiner's principal law. Concretely, this means what 29 out of 30 co-workers want to give the thirtieth one. It is understood that the question of what the thirtieth needs plays a role in this decision (e.g. two families to support, or being forced to live in an expensive apartment). It finds expression in the understanding of the others (29) and not in self justification. Yet other things also become money, such as: that one never appeals in vain to Mrs. Quickly, that Mr. Clever is very lazy, that Mrs. Weepy's ear is open to every pain. The few experiences I am aware off sound quite encouraging. The challenge to judge quite objectively from the point of view of "you" appears to evoke a certain clairvoyant feeling. The fact that in the end, one is No. 30 oneself may support an underdeveloped honesty. If sometimes a notice to leave the school should show up, this should not always be judged as a negative experience. On the other hand, it was impressive that just the very modest, self effacing colleagues became extra thoughtful, of course, within the economic yield.

Yet, if the circle of colleagues should make a misjudgment, it is well to create the possibility of recourse to a revision. Perhaps Mrs. Misery has kept it completely to herself that not only is she a lonely widow, but in addition takes care of her husband's parents. If she tells this to the confidence man – this should preferably not be the treasurer who tends to be tight fisted – he can approach the rights organ. Without divulging Mrs. Misery's secret, he can simply let it be known that, having taken note of Mrs. Misery's situation, he is convinced that her income should be increased by so and so much.

The routine work of the rights organ will probably consist of adding the aspect of the rights life to the wishes that arise from the other organs. These involve the "I and you" in the first place. What is desirable from a pedagogical point of view can have a profound effect on the life of the colleagues. What promises the best economic result can destroy much that is human. Here and nowhere else must these questions be freely discussed, but even here, without connecting the understanding with the judgment of another person. (See appendix B.) One can give the people involved the opportunity to take position in relation to the suggestions from their personal point of view without urging them to do so. Any attempt to force the acceptance of a suggestion with pedagogical necessities or economic pressures must be rigorously forbidden. Everyone knows those factors, because they were present when they were openly debated. The human aspect is the only thing that is being added here.

This is the essential task, yet there is more. It must be investigated whether the suggestion violates rules that one has set for oneself, whether perhaps it is against the bylaws, or whether it is even illegal. Such questions are best referred to a committee, because it is astonishing how many members of a meeting suddenly turn out to be lawyers when typical questions of the law are being discussed. Such expert opinion, by the way, does not prevent the gathering of the rights organ from forming its own judgment.

This brings us to the third main activity, the granting of mandates. (This does not refer to cases where tasks are delegated to outsiders, e.g. to lawyers. In such a case the institution has to maintain the right to step in at any time.) In an institution, and quite particularly in a school, most tasks should be referred to the management of individuals or groups of people. This is not only because all co-workers need not be bothered there with every trifle, namely in all three organs, but for much more important reasons of principle. The system of mandate – i.e. the most personal responsibility of this or that authorized person for groups of tasks – is the human foundation for a threefold structure in the meso-social sphere. We may look upon this as the opposite of the hierarchical structure as practiced in business and above all in the life of the state. There co-workers are rare, and practically nobody ever has a mandate – we find only functionaries. The new way of working together is known as the democratic-republican principle. It is dealt with in a separate chapter.

The bestowing of mandates (authorizations) is to some extent a formality. What is there for the organ of the life of rights to consider, once the spiritual organ proposes that Mrs. Sweetchild is to take over the new first grade? Yet it may be that she lacks a work permit or that it was promised to Mr. Shyboy, when he started three years ago that he would be permitted to start once again with the first grade after the third one. But even as a formality ratification of Mrs. Sweetchild is necessary, because it protects her against the intrusion of others into her sphere of duties. No one, except the organ of rights, can relieve her of her duties prior to completion, even though the pedagogues stand on their heads. There are other mandates that are exclusive affairs of the "rights" (legal) organ. I want to name two, both important for the structure of a school.

Events calling for an immediate decision occur in every school. It is also true that not everything that happens falls under a mandate and that there are things too unimportant to trouble the rights organ. This requires a permanent committee. When vandals break a shed into small pieces, one cannot bother to call a rights conference. A person from the permanent committee will have to decide whether he should first go there in person, call a few strong men, or call the police. And if the whole school buzzes with the rumor that Mr. Warrior had answered last nights complaints by parents against Mr. Papinoko during the parents evening by saying that it had been a capital mistake to hire a "jerk," somebody must be available who, after confirming the truth of the rumor, can instantly furlough Mr. Warrior.

As opposed to such a temporary disposition, there is the definite one involving trifles. A class teacher may have the authority to allow pupils to be absent from school for one day; beyond this the acting faculty chairperson or administrator makes a decision and, in questions of special holiday periods, the legal organ itself. As an example, let us suppose that a mother asks a day off for Lizzie to attend the wedding of a distant relative in the provinces. Should the class teacher say "no", because she fears that this may open the door to a mass exodus, neither appealing to a grievance committee nor to the "rights" organ will help. Those bodies will tell the mother that the class teacher has the right to make such a decision. If the request is for one and a half days, the class teacher would not be allowed to decide this. The grievance committee would probably ask for her opinion. In the same situation the class teachers may find that Lizzie had experienced such a difficult time recently and still worked so very hard that she deserved some happy relaxation. In this case, she makes a pedagogical judgment, yet even as such it must not exceed the one day. At most one could expect that she would not direct the mother to a grievance committee but would involve the latter herself. In case she denies John even half a day off because of his laziness an destructive attitude, the answer to the question as to whether the teacher was right should not consist of some long story but of a short: "We don't deal with this matter."

Such matters must be handled with great consistency: first, in order to slowly penetrate into the secrets of the "I and you" oneself; and second, for the sake of peace – "What do you really have to do with my children?"; third, for pedagogical reasons. Some children have a veritable nose for fuzziness in the authority. I speak from my own experience, having abused this myself when I was myself a Waldorf pupil.

Another mandate job that belongs wholly in the area of the rights organ is that of the supervisor. We have already mentioned this necessity. As emotional beings, humans do not always do what they have found to be right as thinking beings. Hence, it is not enough to have rules; one has to observe them as well. The rights organ must have assigned someone to the job to control adherence to the rules, to point out trespasses to "wrong doers" and, if necessary, to report repeat offenders to the rights organ. This is the supervisor's job, and everyone else is strictly forbidden to raise objections. If they see something obnoxious, they can report it to the supervisor. The job can be shared. It does, for instance, make sense to give this authority to the chairperson of each organ, but only with regard to what happens during a session. Above all else, the mandate should circulate rapidly. No one finds it a pleasant job – and if there is somebody who does, he would not be suitable for it. Everyone should take turns at it, e.g. for three to six months. It is not in itself important how one succeeds in this area. What is important is the knowledge that control exists. Obviously the idea is not to look for offenses.

The supervisor identifies offending deeds or words. He neither judges these nor the person of the offender. This does not even happen if he brings a hopeless case to the plenum. There, only the repeated failure is recorded. More strictly speaking, it is only there one calls behavior unacceptable with a formal vote (counting the votes) or thinks of more far reaching consequences. This means that even the wrongdoer is, even in serious cases, under the protection of the main social rule, namely that the person of the other party is taboo. Only her or his public words and deeds are subject to judgment. This principle, too, and particularly this principle, should be recorded as rule by the organ of the life of rights. See Appendix B regarding this subject. It is a spiritual principle. The rule governs, even though it does not replace the psychological acquisition of social capabilities.

The Decision

Let us survey the structural course of events as based on the above descriptions. The rights organ is asked to act wherever it is desired to nail something down or to make a decision. To the degree that carriers of mandates play a decision-making role, they act as representing the rights organ. Yet, the expert opinions of the spiritual and economic organs and, in the end, of the rights organ are available before a decision can be made. The problem has been illuminated by the same, or almost the same, people from three different, quite one-sided, angles. I have often been asked whether it is possible to judge in opposite ways in the spiritual and rights organs. Practical experience has shown that this is quite easy. In each case one appears in a different mood of soul. This, too, needs to be learned. To be sure, people, and in particular those used to giving orders, make heavy going of this and try to think of economic and legal arguments in favor of their preconceived positions (They usually betray themselves rather quickly, and given that one allows the appropriate facts to be heard in the three organs, they play no significant part in the whole process. Of course, he who wants to be enslaved will find his master.) Only now can everyone claim to be fully informed. Should this not be the case, the rights organ is in a position to decide to run the matter a second and third time through the organs. In the case of very important or specialized questions, external experts will be consulted. (In the life of a school rules are generated whose objective becomes redundant or needs to be adjusted. It helps social hygiene and the sense of justice to re-examine what should be eliminated at, say, biannual intervals. Of course, the elimination of rules requires . . . a decision.)

Isn't this terribly complex? In a certain sense it is. And it is time consuming as well, until one has learned to handle it. In the long run it saves time. After all, one does not solve the three unknowns of three equations all at once, but one after the other, in which case – just as here – practical experience and not principles determines the choice.

Only when all the information is available can a decision be made. What other method of making the decision is possible besides democratic voting? Only if some people are better informed than the rest can there be another method. I will refer to details in chapter 2 and will only summarize in outline: To be democratic does not mean one half plus one voice, but every voice has the same value. One can, however, establish different majorities for different questions. For example, admitting a co-worker should require unanimity, i.e. no vote against. To involuntarily dismiss a co-worker, a qualified majority, for example, two thirds. The latter should also apply to changes of bylaws and for every vote which is questioned by somebody as to whether the decision conforms to the bylaws.

No further discussion precedes the act of decision making. If desired, people should be given an occasion to explain their vote. This explanation, short and to the point, has to be a brief statement why, after weighing all factors, this and no other vote was thought appropriate. If there is enough time, it would be desirable not to come to a vote immediately after the (often rather lively) proceedings in the rights organ. In reality something quite different occurs. What I mean by this is that the three ways of looking at the matter combine themselves to an inner decision, to knowledge of the right solution. By this I mean the call of the voice of conscience. What happens during decision making relates to the considerations like spirit does to soul. The multiplicity of all that the soul had absorbed is needed as a basis. The individual decision – I am for it, or against it – comes from a very different region, namely the night time experience. It is, therefore, beneficial if a night is interposed between the process of consideration and the voting.

It can be very painful if the rights organ decides otherwise, once such a certainty has been arrived at. It can go as far as a person leaving the school. This need not be looked at merely from the negative side. This is where the principal characteristic of threefoldness shows itself in microcosm. The possibility of inner striving is built in, both in the individual case as well as in the whole school. If the three spheres are unable to work together, the institution dies. The co-workers need the challenge that no saving, superimposed authority holds the school together. The fact that a colleague leaves the school because of a decision is one more case of striving and, thus a call to wake up. Yet, if he stays on, he must loyally help carry the decision and accept its consequences. On the other hand, he has earned the right to resubmit the solution that went against his vote, again, to the agenda.

A Board of Trustees?

A school formed on the threefold principle is based on the organic pro and counter action of its three spheres of life. There is no room for a board of trustees. This goes against the ideal of self management. This ideal implies that *all* members take responsibility in the management of the school. The board of directors does not represent the threefold principle but the monolithic state.

Euphemistically speaking, one can call the board of trustees a helping organ for the teachers. This can be true, yet it is never true. For sure, a board of trustees composed of society heavies can impress authorities (and parents?). But is this really what we want? Does not the result of this approach obligate the staff? Can we allow the board of trustees to lose face? And should one believe that board members are indispensable? Would their stature suffer if they would act not as trustees but as deputies of the teachers?

There are far more serious objections against a board of trustees. The board is formally boss and employer. Even if it does not make claim to these prerogatives, its wish becomes command simply because of the board's position. But it will claim them, at the latest when there are crises. No board of trustees will assume the blame for allowing the school to fail. No such body will seriously refuse to listen to parents' complaints. I have experienced again and again that the board of trustees took people to task on issues brought to them by parents. This happened in spite of the arrangement that it was supposed to stay away from pedagogical issues. I have experienced that the teacher representatives within the board of trustees became more and more selective about communicating things that happened in the life of the school. This went on until the bomb exploded, and a very damaging management crisis erupted. I have experienced a case where the board of trustees used a teacher confidant to suggest to a teacher to leave the school without the knowledge of the faculty. This manipulated the faculty into a situation where they had to support the action, if they were to avoid a crisis of the board of trustees. In short, the dirty games we know from politics are thus transferred to the school. Only a " dead board of trustees" is a good board of trustees!

Only if the school is formed as a partnership is there no board of trustees. If, as is usually the case for public relations reasons, a responsible body is required, then there are legal possibilities to eliminate the board of trustees. Every lawyer has the scheme in his closet. The addiction to the management idea has its parallel in the addiction to having a leader of the country. If one really did not want this, not even as a legal prop, one would need only a little mutual trust. Look for trustees who solemnly swear to each other and to the school never to meet as a board, never to interfere in the life of the school in any way. This is how it was done in the Amsterdam Waldorf School. The school acquired the seal of the chairman, and the chairman got the promise that decisions would be communicated to him when the school had reason to believe that he objected to any of these in principle. This was done not so that he could intervene but to allow him to resign in time. This scheme worked to everyone's satisfaction.

    I want to conclude this global discussion of a threefold Waldorf school. I must not fail to prevent a possible misunderstanding. Rules, rights, duties play a relatively large role in this sketch. This may be grist for the mill for those who accuse proponents of the threefold order that they construct rigid formulas instead of describing the living organism. An unfriendly ignoramus could put it this way. In fact, threefoldness *is* the forming principle, and thus one need not be surprised if, in this framework, there is much talk of forms. The threefold order can only guarantee the principle of freedom as a principle of form. For this reason Steiner could call the threefold order the continuation of the **Philosophy of Freedom**. If the structure of a school is in keeping with its time, those who work there can allow *their* pedagogical, social, and economic impulses to flow into it. Any pre-imposed definition of content would deprive the people who carry the actual work. In no way does threefoldness have any say about whether a school practices Waldorf or Montessori pedagogy. All the above examples should be taken merely as elucidation of the structural problems. As a proponent of the threefold order I am not interested in the remark that a school who did not allow Lizzie to take off for her wedding must necessarily be considered as backward. I simply start from the – as far as I am concerned, backward – fact and am interested in its structural consequences. It might not have been absolutely necessary to bring in other structural laws as well to illustrate things. It seems to me that it helps the reader's understanding.

    One should also consider that only the basic features of the structure sketched here are mandatory for a Waldorf school. Practical life makes numerous variations thinkable and often desirable. It may even demand violations. To accept a totally pure model would be dogmatic. Exaggerated purity may even be a method to set the stage for a later triumphal declaration that the threefold order is simply not usable. The point is to know where one wants to go and take every opportunity to get a step closer to the objective. Finally: it is possible to imagine a very different model. Because I know no example of a school, chapter 7 gives a brief sketch of such a model.

Chapter 2

Republican and Democratic

A dictum that is almost taken as a matter of course within the faculties of the Waldorf schools is: a free Waldorf school should be run along republican lines. The origin of this concept is an essay of Ernst Lehrs which first appeared in 1956 but had been kept secreted as " for internal use only". We welcome the fact that it has now been made available to the public as **Republican, not Democratic** in "News from the Anthroposophical Work in Germany," Stuttgart, 1956. The conferences Rudolf Steiner conducted with the first teachers of the Waldorf school are now available in the complete edition (GA 300 a-c). This makes the words of Rudolf Steiner stenographically captured, regarding the structure of the Waldorf school, available as well. This is not unimportant because Lehrs' title covers his point of view without representing the exclusive guideline for the administrative process. Yet, it is ever again used as a practical guideline.

Let us define "republican" in the following way: people with equal rights each administer a specific sector of the institutional life and are individually responsible for this.[1] One could also say that they are true to their statutory objective, in this case: entrusted with a sector, charged with a specific duty, entailing a decision. For example, no teacher can decree that he or she will take over the first grade next year. Such a decision can only be made democratically – everyone has a voice. The decision can also be tackled with the authoritarian principle: one or more persons have the knowledge in contrast to all the others. There is no third alternative. True, one can deliberate until consensus is reached. Either the consensus is genuine, in which case every voice has veto power, or one is allowed to talk, but when the person in charge has stated his or her opinion, the consensus consists of everyone agreeing to the latter.

It has been reported that Steiner originally based the decisions from the teachers' meetings on consensus. He terminated this attempt upon the first incident when a teacher misused it. This would signify, and everyone would agree to it, that consensus is better than decisions based on majority. But consensus is more than not opposing a proposal. Steiner demonstrated this by withdrawing his suggestion in the case in question (GA 300b). To avoid the danger of manipulation, it should be expected of every participant that he/she *bear witness* to his/her concurrence or loyalty vis-à-vis the proposal.

Neither the reported, nor the documented case, allows us to deduce that Steiner considers vote taking appropriate only in case of dishonest motivation. At best, only the initiate can determine this motivation, a situation hardly applicable to a single school in our days. This is quite aside from the thought of whether one should reproach the other person with

---

[1] Regarding the concept republican firstly GA 300a(1975), pg. 68 and GA 293 (1973), pg. 205. Steiner here uses it in contrast to an institutional leadership that emanates from a government or from a Directorate. In a republican conference each person is sovereign, i.e. he or she need not share the point of view of anyone else.

impure motives (see Appendix B). Yet, this is exactly what one does if one demands the taking of a vote.

Vote taking has many enemies. By criticizing my way of looking at it, H.P van Manen appointed himself as spokesman in its favor (see the bibliographic note to chapter 2), although he finds that: "if the staff is not of one mind with a convincing majority . . . , a vote simply must be taken." Yet, he does not wish to rob the staff of the opportunity to arrive at an inspired decision. Needless to say, this possibility depended on whether the individual members of the staff have an active esoteric life, directed toward this objective. At the same time, it goes without saying that one cannot demand this. Yet, if only a single member veers away, the vessel that forms the body of the staff splinters. Anthroposophy calls this vessel *spirit-self.*

It may be that van Manen's proposal can be carried out with an institution with up to ten members. Yet, with the exception of quite rare and structurally insignificant cases of special grace, a halfway mature Waldorf school has a minimum of forty teachers. In this case, it can no longer be done. It is something for the next cultural period – unless one sorts the faculty by esoteric and exoteric groups. In this case, one has introduced a system of two classes, hence something quite antisocial. (See chapter 8 on this subject.) In my work **Anthroposophical Social Impulse** (Schaffhausen 1984, pg. 261), I have shown that, in spite of this, this sort of aiming toward such a vessel is possible today. Chapter 4 provides further elaboration on this subject. Socially, this possibility is subject to strict conditions and is structurally outside the compass of decision making. He who wants to force into being that which lies in the future usually relapses into antiquated conditions. It is the tragic trait of the Waldorf school movement that, in its striving for something unattainable, it performs "human sacrifices." It is the more tragic, if we consider that Rudolf Steiner has given us the remedy.

Should votes be taken in a Waldorf school? Let us turn to the only case where (to my knowledge) Steiner

43

demonstrated the republican-democratic principle. (The proceedings of the 1923/24 Christmas Conferences for the new foundation of the Anthroposophical Society will be set aside because now, more than ever, it remains an open question what Steiner had structurally intended at that time.) I venture to surmise that Steiner's utterance reported by Lehrs accurately fits this case. It has merely been diluted to a catchword in this case.

There existed certain claims for leadership within the Waldorf schools. Steiner wished to block this by having a commission established as a basic function. This formalized and gave continuity to certain administrative aspects which, up to that time, had been bundled together. As opposed to the teaching functions which Steiner bestowed personally, here he wanted that the "triumvirate" would be elected by the colleagues. A more permanent task of coordination and representation was assigned to this body. The procedure he proposed was extremely interesting. In no way were the teachers to elect the three persons. They elected six persons, whom they considered as most capable to identify the three representatives, by written, i.e. secret ballot. This first election then was done along strict democratic principles: every faculty member had a vote, and the six persons with the most votes were elected. (GA 300b)

The next step was to bring the list of six elected persons as a *proposal* to the meeting of the College of Teachers, luckily also in Steiner's presence. I say luckily, because one of the participants, identified with "Y", now proposes to include another person, identified by name, into the triumvirate. Now Steiner pulls out all stops to tell this know-it-all off. The conference at this point has only one possibility, namely to publicly say yes or no to the proposal. It could not be tolerated that one first appoints a nominating committee, the members of which one trusts, and that then one teacher casts a de facto vote of no confidence with his proposal to elect an additional person. This shows nothing less than that the committee had failed to carry its task out in a proper manner. Whatever the poor miscreant said, Steiner attacked more strongly and even made it impossible for him to concede the point. One could almost get the impression that a criminal was being unmasked here.

It may very well be that the emphasis received by this aspect of the case was due to the one-sided stress placed on the republican principle, because this principle is what it was all about. One had entrusted a committee with a task. It could accomplish this task by itself, as long as it had the assurance of the confidence of the conference. No one was entitled to get involved, not even with "good advice." If we assume the conference would have said "no", this would have amounted to no less than a vote of no confidence. In all probability it would have resulted in the members of the committee quitting the school. One could exaggerate and say that the know-it-all had endangered the life of the school. It is my impression that Steiner wanted to impress this fact indelibly into the souls of those present.[2]

This republican aspect should, however, not allow us to ignore the second and democratic event in this affair. The carriers of the mandate were not called by the commission. Its proposal was presented to the staff, and that body – democratically – elected the triumvirate. An election took place. Yet, in this case the democratic principle has a mere formal significance, in contrast to the election of the committee. The proposal ended the task of the committee, and the mandate had been carried out. Since the staff agreed to the proposal, those with a vote had personally accepted the result. This may be seen as a form of exoneration. Should the choice of the triumvirate later prove to have been a mistake, not the committee but every voter would have shared in the responsibility.

---

[2] It is not impossible that Steiner only decided during the appointment process to use this case as an example, because prior to the election he commented: "In the end what has been presented as a proposal will be dealt with within the faculty."

Although it is often the case that — and in fact it happened in this one — the democratic procedure is short circuited by acclamation for accepting the proposal, the possibility to reject it must in principle remain open. Sometimes it is necessary that opinions get split due to some, in itself insignificant, point. This is literally true.

The example I used as a demonstration could, of course, also be used as an emergency solution, especially in cases where behavior threatens the community. One could even support one's procedure by leaning on the wording of the conferences relating to the subject. In my opinion this would misjudge the way Steiner used the procedure. When it comes to the social sphere, one sees again and again how he uses actual cases to feel his way and . . . has the patience to wait for the right case. When such a case arises, the generality is being explained in hand with the actual case.

We can assume that "Case Y" was the first where personal tensions within the faculty came to the surface. Steiner used the case as a tutorial. Even if this tutorial involves only personal tensions, one may well ask: where can we find schools without such tensions? But even if democratic voting were to pertain to cases threatening the community, one may ask oneself who has the right to uncover a colleague's motives and to express a moral condemnation by asking for a vote?

Yet, was Rudolf Steiner indeed against voting? He most certainly was. But he was against money and still had some in his pocket; he even created a theory of money in the same way as, in our case, a guideline for democratic practice.

The democratic and the republican principles are polar opposites. The more one delegates the responsibility for different areas, the less of substance exists that needs democratic decisions. By delegating tasks one has also given up the right to decide. As far as the delegated mandates are concerned, the working community has renounced the right to a democratic relationship to the particular mandate. This is, of course, an advantage if, as a result, the general meeting no longer needs to concern itself with every trifle. It is also good if the initiative and responsibility in the delegated field increase. Yet if one goes too far, the coordination toward the institutional objective erodes – a disadvantage. Every person administers his/her own areas.

One can also turn it around as follows: the creation of coordinating functions is a sign that the equilibrium between the democratic and republican principle is disturbed. There are insufficient occasions to test each individual's course against the course of the institution and, if need be, make democratic decisions to achieve adjustments. Things get to be very questionable when areas of authority are delegated for longer periods, i.e. when the continuation of mandates becomes a formality (done by acclamation). In this case power structures with a bureaucratic aspect are formed within the organization. Their way of functioning no longer has anything to do with "democratic" or "republican" but rather with an authoritarian regime. One year is more than long enough for most mandates. The statutes should call for automatic retirement after that. The function (not the carrier of the mandate) should automatically be subjected to re-evaluation before one elects a new carrier of the mandate (by secret ballot). Exceptions are possible and sometimes technically required. The best example is the class teacher of the lowest grade in a Waldorf school who normally receives a mandate for eight years!

In its formal aspect the republican principle may almost be called arrogant due to its unapproachability. It, therefore, needs to be supplemented on the human level. Although it prohibits unwanted interference, it in no way prevents the carrier of the mandate from asking for advice or help. Often there will be a great need for this. One can seek a confidant, one can form a circle of advisors, and one can even turn to the general assembly for help – all this is possible, as long as it originates from the carrier of the mandate. But all this is just as impossible if it originates from others, even if it is meant as "friendly advice." "If I were you, I would talk with X," is rude interference, because it expresses a criticism. It must be well noted that the *"called for"* help, whether advice or assistance, does not, even by a single iota, reduce the personal responsibility.

In the case of mistakes, uncertainty, etc., the threshold for asking the advice of a colleague is lower to the degree that the carrier of a mandate can be certain that no busybody intends to disqualify or hurt him or her. Not only has this a positive effect regarding the problem in question, but it also has a socially healing effect and, in the end benefits coordination. One learns to feel where, within one's own domain, one need not always shoot to kill.

Similarly, too much democracy undermines the institution. The meetings turn into nightmares if the plenum has to decide whether Mary can take an afternoon off, whether a new typewriter should be purchased, whether an announcement in the school paper should be rejected. Meetings get to be more and more poorly attended, and boredom makes people push pet projects. Such signs of fatigue are often a sign of too much democracy.

In Anthroposophical matters the republican principle is routinely used to a great extent, and although it is quite rarely being adhered to with total consistency, there is no reason to belabor it further. This does not apply to the democratic principle; therefore, I want to illuminate a few more aspects of the same.

The democratic principle is reduced to a farce, if the chairman of the meeting puts an end to the discussion with the words: "no one against? – then the proposal is accepted." In such a case one can predict with perfect certainty that should the consequences of the decision be unfavorable, one would hear from many sides: "I never agreed with this." One is shortchanging democracy by thinking that it is merely a matter of majorities. It is also and foremost a matter of *taking note of the votes*. The procedure used in the meeting and the way it is being handled should be aimed toward a situation where one stands up for one's opinion or, as a minimum makes it heard. The "yes" or "no" should come from the will. It should be an audible word, a raised hand, a written position.

And the will is answered by the falling gavel: this was *your* decision.

This is why votes should be counted, even in the presence of a clear majority, specifically with "for," "against," and "no vote." One should check whether the number of votes coincides with the number of recognized voters present. (GA 300b) It should be made clear to the voters what it means to cast no vote, namely not : "I don't know yet and will see what position I take as things go along." Not casting a vote means either "I don't care whether it is yes or no", or "In this matter I lack the ability to judge, and, therefore, I accept the point of view of the majority." He who does not want the latter must vote against the proposal.

It is also part of democracy to cast secret votes in the case of one participant wishing this or when the chairman feels that there are people who lack the courage to voice their opinion. It is certainly true that in the age of the consciousness soul everybody should stand by his or her opinion, yet one cannot demand this of anyone. One can make it easier for such people and hope that their courage will increase as time goes on. When people are being chosen, the secret procedure should be routine, as Steiner demonstrated in our example. Here it is not only a matter of courage, it is a matter of the china.

The democratic principle is often unjustifiably being identified with "half + 1." Democratic formally means no more than that all the votes count equally and have equal weight. Nowadays there should be no more animals under the law who are "more equal" than other animals (Orwell's *Animal Farm*). But what majority is needed to accept a decision is another question. Here there exists no basic rule; it is a question of agreement. The latter should be fixed by statute or by written procedure. The meeting can easily be manipulated if the decision is made that for each individual case, a simple majority, two thirds of the votes, or unanimity is needed.

"Consensus" is a beautiful rule which has ruined many an institution. It is a go ahead for gripers. In spite of this, there are areas where it is desirable. I have the acceptance of a new member with the right to vote in mind.[3] The vote of this person will make (contribute to) future decisions not only about the well-being of the institution, but also about each individual co-worker as well. In this respect a school is not different from a corporation under civil law. If the statutes do not make an exception, the acceptance of a new partner is possible only with the consent of all partners of record at that time. This is a good rule for a Waldorf school as well, even though here there is no fortune to invest and no profit motive.

The condition of unanimity is undesirable if one must, or wishes to, let go a co-worker. This would place everyone in a position of power. Very few people indeed are immune to the seduction of the latter. A blockhead could make it impossible to resolve a crisis. There are other ways to avoid emotional decisions. Within the democratic sphere one may consider a recess in the proceedings or a statutory condition that says layoffs of co-workers with a vote require, let us say, a three-quarter majority.

A qualified majority is not only desirable in the case of changes in the statutes, but every time when even a single qualified voter questions the statutory acceptability of a decision. For example: does the set objective of the Waldorf school – pedagogically based on the spiritual science of Rudolf Steiner – allow teaching the children to work with multiple choice questions? Although here unanimity would not be the right thing, due to the usual block of people with pet ideas, it may still be wise not to make a decision if even one co-worker has serious qualms about this.

---

[3] A vote should only be given to a person who will accept the consequences of his or her decisions in extreme cases all the way to personal bankruptcy. This is why the democratic principle is incompatible with the system of salaries - one more reason why it has become inappropriate for out time. There should exist only an association of "free entrepreneurs" or something similar to this.

AWSNA Publications

Finally – here we return to our point of departure – delegating authority should also require qualified majorities. One should demand a widely based vote of confidence for the very reason that in institutions based on Anthroposophy, the emphasis is fully on the republican principle. Anyone whose sphere of authority is granted based on a small majority will certainly feel insecure. Being elected is not enough. One also needs to be recognized "by the free understanding of one's co-workers right down to the last laborer." (GA 329)

In the institutional life, and especially in areas of the spiritual life, democracy will always have to be a subordinate matter. Whatever is being contributed to the social structure, with the help of an organization in the economic or spiritual spheres, invariably depends on the abilities of human beings, and, thus, on the latitude they are given (republican principle). It is a matter of the coffee, not of the cup. But the cup is essential, and even a crack can have painful consequences. Anyone who refuses the existence of any trace of democracy in his institute naturally looks for the cause for anything that goes wrong in the human sphere in the evil nature or incompetence of his or her subordinates, if not in inflammatory writings of irresponsible critics. Yet, the visitor of institutions who has an eye for structures will find everywhere the – often catastrophic – consequences of sloppy procedures, usually as regards the democratic component. This is due to the fact that their elimination does not lead to a strengthening of the republican principle but to a relapse into hierarchical conditions. The College meeting is replaced by an intangible, informal, and, above all, content devouring power.

Van Manen's proposal, mentioned above in connection with his speech in opposition to my point of view also courts this danger. He proposed changing the function of the organ, nowadays usually called the "executive committee of the College of Teachers", in which the leading teachers make the decisions vital to the school. According to this proposal, the organ is changed to become a council of experienced persons who helps the carriers of mandates with advice as the need arises. Such a counseling arrangement for undecided carriers of mandates will unavoidably develop into a "gray eminence" – a dictator who rules behind the scenes – (from "*Eminence Grise*," a French archbishop who virtually ruled France in the days prior to the French revolution.) In each case of disagreement with the way the mandate is handled, the condemning question would arise: "Why was the organ of experts not consulted?" Not only does this prevent "Lone Rangerism" and "Formation of Fractions", it also more importantly constrains the freedom of the carrier of the mandate to seek advice from those in whom alone he has confidence in this specific case. I abstain from judging how van Manen's suggestion relates to the pedagogical impulse.

I certainly do not wish to criticize established customs in Waldorf schools with the above remarks. Whoever is fond of them should use them or be used by them. One should only be aware of the fact that, in this case, one is acting in contradiction to the threefold social order. This book is meant to provide a clear picture. An institution may serve Anthroposophical objectives to whatever degree it wishes. However, as long as it does not strive to realize the impulse toward social structure within those objectives, it is not an Anthroposophical *institution*.

In our time human beings are ever less willing to subordinate themselves to the interests of associations. In spite of this wherever social life is being organized and assumes an institutional character, it is impossible to avoid subjugation to the objective of the institution. We must live with this paradox. It also lives in contradictory remarks in the work of Rudolf Steiner. We find a way of living with it, when we accord an area of freedom to the individual co-worker (republican principle), but only when the authority to direct, connected to this area (delegation) – and formulation and interpretation of the objectives as well – is based on the consensus of everybody (democratic principle). In this way one is not governed by others, but subordinates oneself to one's own decision of accepting the closely defined mandate.

Lehrs' essay has contributed in a very one-sided manner to a republican orientation in schools.[4] This is partly due to the title and probably also due to the author's personal preference for republicanism. One does not, however, violate the sociological law without penalty. This is how, in many cases, the rudder was placed into the hands of the manager instead of in the hands of the republicans.

---

[4] In *Round Letter to the Teachers* 1971/2, Lehrs published a synopsis of his article. The introductory words of this letter clarify his position. His battle against democracy is solely based on democratic interference with an existing mandate. Here I am even more radical than he, because I too, reject unasked for advice as interference. But, democracy, as such, is then degraded to an appendage of the republican principle without giving examples and without further considerations. This position ignores the meaning of democracy within the meso- threefold order in general as well as within the four democratic votes Steiner intiated on January 31, 1923. "There are more areas of disagreement between Lehrs and myself. As an example an expression like 'Hierarchy of Functionaries' is foreign to my ideas. 'Democratic Structure of a Republic' would come closer to this. Here I must confine myself to pointing to the tragic and structural necessity of majority decisions in terms of my 'Anthroposophical Social Impulse.' "

AWSNA Publications

Chapter 3

The Legal Committee

When we discuss this organ, we go beyond the boundaries of the school. We are forced to go beyond them, because this organ is based on the social law that no one can be the judge in his own affairs. This means that in cases where the school is party to a conflict, it should not pronounce the judgment. This is a matter of course in a state governed by law. In case of conflicts between private persons and organizations, the independent judge can be used as a resource. He would also be available to judge cases meant for the legal committee. Yet, it would be wrong simply to assume that he possesses the understanding for the conflict before him. This unnecessarily increases the possibility for a wrong judgment.

We refer to conflicts where private interests collide with interests of organizations. An example of a common and obvious case: The rights organ wishes to separate a teacher. The latter does not wish to leave, be it because he finds this unacceptable in his present situation ("Where can I go at 56 years of age?"), be it that he finds the separation pay too low, ("Then you will have to take care of me as well!"), that letting him go is not in the interest of the school ("You do this only because I have a misunderstanding with the Anthroposophical Society."), etc. One could, indeed, go to a professional judge with questions such as these. But should such a person judge what is expected of a Waldorf teacher? A second body of conflicts involves the question whether the school, in its efforts, has remained within its statutory goals. Imagine that the rights organ bows to controversial conditions with a $^2/_3$ majority in order not to lose state subsidies. When one's own income is in danger, goals are sometimes interpreted in a rather generous manner, and conscience develops loopholes. Should a scandalized teacher ask the professional judge to decide whether a test falls under the statutory definition of "Pedagogy according to Rudolf Steiner," if one has to lie in order to pass? No doubt many a legal question goes beyond the competence of the judge, regardless of how often his experience has allowed him to make wise decisions.

In general, the complexity of today's society has resulted in referring conflicts to specialized arbitrators rather than to professional judges. This applies to Waldorf schools as well. The latter should bear in mind Rudolf Steiner's suggestion that the judges should be in place long before any conflict occurs. Once a conflict exists, each party looks for an arbitrator – preferably a rather forceful one – whom they know shares his/her point of view. In this case, it is likely that the result will be a compromise, rather than a decision, that satisfies one's sense of justice. I outline the chief features of an organ of rights without addressing the details of its derivation as follows:

The judges or arbitrators to be elected should fulfill three requirements:

1. Every member of the staff should have at least one arbitrator in the organ whom he trusts to such an extent that he would have enough confidence in him or her to make him judge in his own affair, should it come to it.

2. Only persons who are trusted by *all* members of the staff to be objective should be candidates for the job. It is almost impossible to satisfy this requirement, if arbitrators are only elected when conflicts arise.

3. No staff members, past or present, should be elected because they are much too involved with the interests of the school. The arbitrators should preferably be people active in the school movement in the widest sense of the word, i.e. with much experience of school problems, for example, retired teachers from other schools.

AWSNA Publications

This may give the impression that a school with a staff of 60 needs 50 arbitrators, if the first two requirements are to be met. This is so in theory, yet my experience has been that the staff in Amsterdam needed only six arbitrators for 45 teachers, because the same names kept reoccurring on the ballots (first requirement), and because there was no objection against any of the six (second requirement). There appears to be a high degree of consensus as to who is trustworthy and deserves to be a judge. In contrast to this, I would like to mention our experience with the election of arbitrators, which we held, more or less as an exercise, with the students of our course on the threefold order. It was formally meant as a case to cover difficulties that are likely when it comes to the interpretation of the educational contract between students and docents. This being a new area led to a situation where the forty students needed fifteen judges. Even this number was reached after so many complaints that one had a hard time finding new names. This shows that a certain body of experience with the area involved is indispensable and cannot be expected from students who have just arrived from all points of the compass.

The question may arise whether other people, e.g. parents involved with the school, should be included in this process of arbitration. I think that this can be done to a limited extent only. It is simply not appropriate to entrust the choice of the arbitrator to parents, who are frequently unacquainted with the essence of Waldorf schools. The professional arbitrator would be better prepared to do this. Additionally, it is simply a practical impossibility to keep asking over and over again whether confidence in the established arbitrators exists, as parents change from year to year. But in case of quarrels, one can volunteer to give parents the choice to use the legal committee. In this case, one has to eliminate its right to invoke a civic judge. This may sometimes be useful. Parents who bring their child to the Waldorf school with great conviction and indeed have absorbed the basic ideas of Waldorf education, may at times be irritated to have what is here sold as Waldorf pedagogy judged by a committee of experts.

It may be clear to everyone that one has to handle the statute with care. A two-thirds majority, considered to be within the framework of the statute for a decision that needs to be taken, may be cause for the teaching staff to refer to the legal committee when very serious reservations exist. On the other hand, when one feels that a colleague has reservations based on his conscience, it may be wise to put the decision on ice, even if the necessary majority voted for it. Is it not true that one person often functions as conscience for an initiative gone amok. One cannot assume that outsiders will hesitate to invoke the statute without hesitation. If one wanted to provide proof that everything the school does is based on Steiner's pedagogy, one would wind up with a legalistic lifestyle that suffocates any spiritual life. This is why one should limit the right to object to what in administrative law is called "limited testing." It is not a matter of whether a decision **is** Waldorf pedagogy, but whether one has the right to consider it to be within this framework without stretching the concept of Waldorf (or Steiner) pedagogy beyond its limits.

Once the arbitrators have been elected and have accepted their office, one can only hope that they will never be needed. When a conflict should arise, however, everyone should have the right to designate any member of the board as judge. This member need not be the one whom the person in question had originally in mind as his/her confidential judge. If the two arbitrators of the contending parties cannot arrive at unanimity, they can involve a third member of the board.

Perhaps one cannot repeat the procedure whenever a new member joins the staff. This really does not matter. It even has the advantage that novices have to accept the existing board of judges for two or three years. Yet, at no more than three year intervals, one should make sure that the requirements for confidentiality are still assured for all members of the staff. It should be a condition for admittance of new staff members that, in the case of quarrels, they will undertake

AWSNA Publications

to accept the judgment of the chosen judges and waive the involvement of the professional arbitrators.

Chapter 4

The Spiritual Organ

In his "Politeia" Plato makes the philosophers rule, yet only after they reach the age of fifty. According to Plato, it is only then that they have become wise enough. This saying can be helpful, like much that stems from the time before Christ, if we turn it around. After the age of fifty, a human being should no longer assume a position of authority.

Humans who have reached the highest level of their epoch have also reached the apex of their personality. One should eliminate everything that limits their freedom as much as possible. The threefold order is, among other things, based on this impulse. If a person must be exposed to the impressive sayings of a wise person day in and day out, his/her freedom is constrained. This is particularly true at the time of younger persons' most intensive activity in the outer world. I am not talking about a Solomon or Socrates, but simply someone who, over the years, has gathered more wisdom than a younger person. This problem of age is similar to the one of function which we have encountered in the basic structure. In case of the latter, one needs to guard the economic or legal impulse against the overbearing influence of the know-it-all. It is only quite natural that the older person cannot be expected to have much understanding of the new initiatives of younger persons – granted that young ones are often impetuous and rash. We need not even think of our postwar octogenarians who have made Europe a breeding place for catastrophes with their sclerotic ideas.

This condition gets worse when the senior members assume structural key positions, which is often the case, because they are so capable. In actual practice, their word then becomes a command. In a school they are often found as chairs of the organs, on the permanent board, on the building committee, as teacher representative on the board of directors, on the curriculum committee, as representatives on the school committee, as godfather of a new foundation, etc. One considers them as indispensable – a view they share. None of this is directed against the younger members. As this can have primarily social consequences, one needs to observe great care in this area. Aggression or subservience result where there is no room for personal initiative . Both are equally dangerous for a school, even though the former is more visible.

I know that these words are unfair to many a senior person. There are many examples of wonderful, wise persons who gradually disengage from their involvement, who are wise enough to be silent and never try to play the first fiddle. We are once more faced with a fundamental social tenet. We cannot allow one person to do what we allow the other. The latter would certainly and justifiably feel wounded in their dignity. Legal rules must be valid without reference to the individual. Know-it-alls, to whom personality is everything, suspect such rules for that very reason. They, too, will have to get used to the fact that the social sphere is governed by principles that differ from the ones that govern the spiritual or economic life. Indeed, we are surrounded by this in our daily lives. The fact that the consciousness of Mr. Beerbelly is not affected by his indulgence in drink does not eliminate a legal alcohol "maximum per mil. law." Even Mr. Beerbelly will have to abide by it (unnecessarily, of course).

It would surely be best if a school would create its own rule that as people on the staff reach their fiftieth year, they have to withdraw from all but their pedagogical mandates. As a rule, history makes this impossible. In this case, the question of curbing the "founders" gets to be an increasing problem. What makes it even more difficult is the fact that the seniors are capable of contributions vital to the further development of the school(s). After all, they really do possess wisdom.

Our older heroes usually lose this wisdom, when it comes to judging their own effect on the younger generation. They forget how they suffered from the pressure of those who were old when they were young. They used to groan when they discovered it impossible to get around Mr. Sittingbull or Mrs. Knowitall, when someone had to be appointed to this or that board.

I would like to point out two ways to profit from the wisdom of the elders without negative side effects.

It would be of great value for the school movement, if these experienced teachers would coach the younger generation, but never in their own school. In one's own school good advice looks like a command, even if it is not meant in this way. Within one's school, one is on guard to make sure the mentor does not become aware of one's weaknesses. Who knows how this can sometimes be used against one? In another school, this is quite different. Here the coach is the good uncle whose advice leaves one free – as opposed to a father's advice. Again, this is not so, if the mentor is forced on the inexperienced member of the faculty whose pedagogy is still weak. Here is a task for old age that goes far beyond activities in one's own school. It cannot be imposed, because nobody wants to sentence a meritorious old pedagogue to a nomadic existence. One can also be content with the essence of pedagogical work in one's own school. If someone has this wisdom, the colleagues discover that he really no longer cares about administrative questions, and no longer allows himself to judge the work of colleagues. In this case, people will come one by one and ask for advice. The wisdom of old age can issue forth in a creative manner. It is possible to go a step further and make this way of being there for others an organic part of the school.

A circle of teachers – and at times even a human being who belongs to the periphery – comes together when a Waldorf school is taking shape. This group acts out of inspiration. The initiative is not just carried by humans. Spiritual beings act through them – quite often even a departed person who has died during the time of the school's founding. In these founders one can experience something like an ideal image that anticipates what is trying to incarnate in time. If one of these is driven out, it is deadly for the school, because they are the portal through which the spiritual world is working. Only as a group together do they form a vessel that can be used by the spiritual world to give a helping hand to a spiritual concern.

The spiritual stream dries up during the second bureaucratic phase.[5] As far as the original basic impulse is concerned, one feeds on the past. With the new form the founders themselves become a problem. They are not consolidators. In sociology this is a well known subject, but unknown to most institutions. As a result, one is not prepared for it. Two lifestyles clash against each other. This period usually lasts quite a long time. To overcome it would be desirable if the founders would withdraw from their task of exercising willpower outwardly to a meditative inner one. Of course, one cannot ask for this.

This inner task would involve letting the events of the school pass by the soul in cyclic images with a very specific inner attitude. Whatever can be perceived as positive within the life of the school should be ascribed to the colleagues, and everything that went wrong to one's own shortcomings. This is no caricature of reality; spiritually observed it really looks

---

[5] I refer the reader to my book *The Anthroposophical Social Impulse*, where I give a detailed description of the three phases: the founding phase, the bureaucratic phase, and phase of communication. I would only like to add that this description concerning phase 1 and 2 agrees in all but minor points with Lievegoed's concept (e.g. in *Social Formations On Hand Of The Example Of Curative Pedagogic Arrangements* Frankfurt 1986). We differ regarding the third phase which, however, can hardly be deduced from practical experience at this time, but whose picture can be read in the social demands of our time.

like that. If one encounters each other in this way, something can come to life among the founders to form a chalice into which the stream of inspiration can flow again. The *cosmic* wisdom Sophia enters in.

Don't expect that the newly found, fertile knowledge has to precipitate to the members of the circle of elders. Their circle is the chalice for the school. The content, captured here, can inspire every colleague. Routine work will bring about increasing growth and substantial knowledge about the school on the part of the members in spite of this. Thus, they will be in a position to react to events in a more spiritual manner. This creates the danger that, even more than due to their age, their preponderance becomes overwhelming. One could call such a circle esoteric, because it really has only this function. Therefore, the conditions for membership in it must include the stipulation to refuse every mandate that implies a voice in any matter within one's own school. Of course, it is no problem to be a teacher and also no problem to work within interscholastic committees. Secondly, discussions of solutions of problems that surfaced in the school should be avoided at all cost within these circles. The danger exists that an unnamed group governs the school from behind an impenetrable curtain, a gray eminence based on gray magic. One could speak of the evil counter-image of the chalice.

Finally, the following may be added concerning the members of this spiritual circle. Most certainly one is not assigned to this due to one's occult powers. Not all founders are geniuses. Some of them may even have their limitations. But since it is a spiritual entity, one is part of it as a spiritual being. Here all of us are equal. Competitive attempts to achieve leadership destroy the circle. The aging founders are usually the logical members. One need not, however, limit oneself to them. But the members should be few. Certainly no more than ten. This is not because any meditative conversation cannot otherwise arise – there is no limit, but for the simple sober reason that one should arrange it so that every member can participate. This brings us to the next desirable thing: if a member leaves the circle, changes the school, retires, or dies – look for a successor. But look for someone who is as like to the departed member in spiritual stature as possible in order to close the hole in the spiritual chalice in the best possible way. It would be spiritually appropriate if the successor would refrain from imbuing the place of the departed member with his own personality but rather represent the essence of that person, in as far as it is within his or her powers. Of course, this would only apply within the circle. Such a sacrifice would enhance the impersonal character of the circle, which is demanded vis-à-vis the spiritual world.

Chapter 5

The Waldorf School and Waldorf School Parents

The relationship between parents and the school is a reoccurring cause of friction. This is understandable. Some parents, dissatisfied with public schools or schools run by religious confessions, have looked for a Waldorf school. Such parents, in particular, are not indifferent toward pedagogy, and, therefore, often wish to follow the way teachers deal with their children. They may be quickly perceived as uncomfortable nuisances and treated accordingly. On the other side of the coin, teachers often display demands (urgent requests) toward the home, which potentially infuriate the parents.

This chapter is meant to describe the points of contact between parents and school and examine how potentially conflicting points of view may be dealt with in a way that allows discussion between the two parties, without relegating one of them to the role of mere spectator. In dealing with this, we cannot use the procedure of conventional school systems as our approach to this problem. This would only result in a patchwork of misunderstandings, fixed ideas, dogmas, and resentments. We must start from the threefold structure of the school and deal with the relationship with the parents from this point. The cause of conflicts really does not lie in the unwillingness or in the inadequacy of one of the parties, but in the absurd role forced on both parties by an absurd structure.

If a school wants to work on the basis of Anthroposophical didactic and pedagogy, it should form its life based on the threefold social order. Freedom in the sphere of the spirit, equality in the sphere of rights, and brotherliness in the economic sphere should reign in such a school. From this point of view, one can identify three points of contact with the parents. These are by their nature very different from each other. The contact line created by the sphere of the spirit will concern us in the first place, because a school's educational activities are based on that sphere.

Spiritual freedom is clearly the most developed area of a Waldorf school. If all is well in this area, every teacher is free to proceed with her or his task of education in his/her own way. This means that neither parents nor colleagues, and least of all a board of trustees, have a right to give directions. The first potential conflict can be identified in this area. Both parents and teachers work with the same child as educators (often other persons as well, such as the religious instructor, a music teacher, a sports teacher, but we can ignore those for our discussions). This is so self evident in school life that one hardly realizes how unusual this situation is in non-institutional life. There it seldom occurs. For instance, one could think about two physicians treating the same patient. Generally, we have little experience with the tensions in such a situation.

It can hardly be avoided that there are teachers who find that their educational work is being spoiled at home, and parents who feel that their child is either wrongly treated or misunderstood at school. This even happens with one and the same person. A former Waldorf school teacher called his child Waldorf school damaged. This contrast is inherent in school life and creates the danger that one slides down to the sphere of rights: the right of the parents set against the right of the school, based on the acceptance of the pupil.

The original cause for the battle for educational dominance goes back very far and can only be hinted at here. Until the late 19th century, the rule was that those areas of spiritual life, considered affairs of basic world-view, were taken care of by the authorities in a binding manner. As for religion, the motto in Europe was for the longest time: "Who owns the kingdom owns the religion." Education still has to wait for its full emancipation. On the threshold of the third millennium the above point of view has still not really been overcome. The state has reserved the right to form the children after its own pattern, and the parents imitate the state in areas the latter does not wish to enter.

A new insight slowly and gently wants to break through in our time: the realization that the child has a right to its *own* development, that it is inappropriate to force it into social models or desiderata or to tame it into social usefulness. Additionally, we are only beginning to understand that human dignity is injured if we force others, in this case teachers, to teach children something that goes counter to their own conviction. Yet, this is exactly what is demanded by the authorities and by certain parents. The state puts down learning targets (final exam, etc.), and the teacher has to see to it that the demanded knowledge is achieved. In consonance with this, the parents think that the child has to learn this or that, without asking themselves whether any of it goes counter to the teachers' conscience regarding pedagogy or content. They also fail to consider whether what is demanded helps or hinders the personal development of the pupil, whether the teacher can stand up for the content of what is being taught, and finally, whether the method of thinking is acceptable from a pedagogical point of view. Nowadays only a few pioneers are concerned with this group of questions.

We can no longer justify placing all blame on the outlived theory that specialists are best able to judge what a pupil needs for our educational policies. This was still true during the first half of our century. Today the human being is being looked upon as a sort of machine that has to be well programmed in order to achieve certain macro-social and, in particular, macro-economic results. The specialists are carefully chosen by the authorities and have taken over quite different functions than formerly. They exist to throw sand into the eyes of those incorrigible "primitives" who still consider the human being to be an individual. This view of the world contains just as little truth as the world of computers. Whatever helps to achieve a particular objective is true. A legislator who determines, or lets determine, the content of the curriculum is basically identical to O'Brian in Orwell's 1984: "If the majority of people say that twice two equals five, then twice two **is** five."

It was necessary to mention this, not in order to clarify what is so radically different in Waldorf pedagogy – others are better equipped to do this – but because of the prevalent lack of understanding of the consequences of this approach. Here we talk of the *art* of education, not because we wish to claim a higher order of activity, but to make it clear that just as an artist does not create from higher rules and prescriptions, but from very personal insights, the teacher, too, must act with undisturbed autonomy in the creative moments of pedagogical activity. It could be that every colleague shrugs their shoulder about Mr. Somebody's methods, yet none of them have the right to call him to order. "Unless. . .", but that comes later. What if Mr. Somebody makes grave pedagogical mistakes? For sure this is quite possible, but there exists no resource within the authority to judge this. (Pure) spiritual life knows no judges, no written scientific lore either, not even Rudolf Steiner's, except perhaps the golden rule attributed to him, namely: it is not too bad to make mistakes if one makes them out of conviction. The power of inner conviction has more pedagogical value than schematic knowledge (truths).

The parents are on a collision course with this autonomy of the Waldorf teacher. "This is *my* child, and *my* pedagogical conviction tells me that this particular teacher is wrong in the way he treats my child." The above makes it clear that the only target for the parents is the wrongdoer (the teacher), him or herself. If he or she cannot be convinced, one has exhausted all possibilities. It is weak comfort that this autonomy of the teacher applies in even stronger measure to the colleagues. Unasked, they cannot even offer him or her advice. If the parent's complaint is being accepted by a grievance committee or even by the board of directors, this would fuel the emotions on both sides. Those people would be in no position to help the parents, and their soothing tirades would only enrage them beyond measure. (Of course, this does not exclude the possibility that it might be wise on the part of a teacher who receives many complaints from parents to confidentially ask one of his colleagues: ". . . Is there something wrong with me?")

It is well to be very clear about this from the start, if parents bring their child to a Waldorf School. There exists no pedagogical rights authority, only pedagogical partners for pedagogical problems. "Unless. . . ." But the parents should also know just as clearly that the reverse of this is also true. The highest authority for the child's education at home is the parents. "Unless. . . ."

Let me mention something else about the education from both sides before we discuss the threefold "unless. . . ." The awkwardness in dealing with these problems has led to many experiments. These had very strange results, such as the parents' council. The ideas generated in this area follow the democratic model too closely, which is quite unsuitable for the spiritual life. To put it a bit too plainly, this model results in the minorities always being in the right. The autonomy enjoyed by both teachers and parents does not exclude counseling sessions. It is even anchored in the structure of the

Waldorf school that the teacher should bring these about. Unfortunately, the house visit is only too often under time constraints. It should not only provide a picture of the pedagogical atmosphere at home, it should also provide an opportunity to discuss educationally desirable issues without sacrificing either party's autonomy. As already mentioned, the "parents evening" should primarily be dedicated to the needs of parents and teachers, i.e. it should deal with economic issues. One should avoid dealing with principles of education or with the educational problems of a specific child. If the opportunity is offered, it could be practical for parents to talk with teachers of special subjects about their child, because such teachers make no house visits. It might be a reason for the parents energetically to help participate in the improvement of these structurally created counseling opportunities, because they are not always satisfactory. If the teacher shows unwillingness, or if he fills the time with platitudinous talk, then there is reason to complain to the rights organ. The teacher violates the school's own structure. Here we touch one of the "unless. . ." items. The teacher may very well be autonomous, but this gives him or her no right to put him or herself above the school structure. We shall return to this.

It depends on their social capabilities whether the discussions between parents and teachers have a result. We may assume that neither party wishes to make the child become a victim of the conflict. A very good pedagogue often sees possibilities to meet the parents' wishes, because he knows of a sufficient number of methods to counteract possible damaging results. In his despair, a weak pedagogue would more easily tend to elevate his autonomy to a power tool.

I would like to cite an example from practical life. A mother, an anthroposophist for many years, had moved to a particular city in order to give her children a Waldorf education. Both motivation as well as knowledge of the background of Waldorf pedagogy were present. Her son Simon was very hard of hearing and otherwise normal. The teacher assigned Simon a place next to a deaf youngster. The mother appeared right away and requested another place for her son. He needed to concentrate very hard to understand the lesson. This was impossible for him, because his neighbor continually interrupts with "what did he say?" The teacher saw this in an entirely different light. For Simon this exact place was pedagogically right, because nobody could have more understanding for a deaf person than one who was hard of hearing. And besides, the pedagogical concern went beyond that which passed through the ear. The conflict escalated. In our context it was unimportant who was declared to be right. It is important that there existed two mutually exclusive pedagogical approaches. In an extreme case this can lead to the child leaving the school.

Could parents not join forces and proceed together in specific cases, for example, if a weakness of a teacher is commonly felt? Does this perhaps present a task for class parents? This would lead from one evil to another. Every child is unique, and therefore the parents can intercede only for their own child. From a pedagogical point of view the other children are none of their business. And if the power of the crowd is going to replace the arguments, this would irritate anyone who is truly placed in the life of the spirit. Yet there is no reason why parents cannot help each other to overcome their timidity. "Why don't you speak to Mr. Anybody and point out to him our concerns? I will do it, too."

Parents and school meet each other in a totally different way in the sphere of rights. It is an underdeveloped area, which usually comes to the fore at the wrong time and in the wrong way. The hairsplitting that goes on in cases of conflict is peripheral to the sphere of rights, just like the tricks, bordering on downright swindle, in the sphere of economics. Parents should be aware of the fact that they have a threefold relationship of rights vis-à-vis the school.

1. If one enrolls one's child in the school, a (verbal or written) contract is present. This contract covers more than the amount of tuition! It is, in the first, place a declaration of the will. The school promises to engage itself for the child in

the field of education. The parents promise to engage themselves to facilitate the task of the school. The parents' contributions are only one part of this. Child and parent become members of an organization by this contract and have to adapt themselves to the organization. What particular commitments the school imposes should be worked out by each school in a set of school regulations. The parents should be asked to sign this document. Anything verbally agreed upon during an acceptance interview may be formally equal to a written contract, yet in case of a conflict experience shows that verbal agreements are always vigorously contested by both sides.

Such a contract is neither insignificant nor one-sided. Of course, parents cannot expect that the school regulations will be changed for them and their children. But they acquire rights from the contract, even if to be free in all things not laid down by the contract. It should never occur that the school adds supplemental regulations at a later date. Parents can successfully defend themselves against this. These school regulations include in the first place the demands the school makes on the behavior of the pupil outside the school: smoking, television, drugs, to name a few actual demands. The timing and reasons for terminating the contract with the school should also be accurately defined. A contract, including one involving school regulations, is an agreement between two parties. Neither party is allowed to change it unilaterally, although the schools often depart from this. As concerns the parents, one is obligated to obtain the agreement of every pair of parents if one wishes to change the school regulations.

This is a touchy subject. We must make a careful distinction between regulations and pedagogical measures. As regards the latter, as much freedom as possible should prevail, if not absolute freedom, as we shall see under 2 below. Yet how often are regulations packaged as pedagogical measures? I have experienced a teaching staff who had obtained confirmation from the school council that the introduction of the school-free Saturday was needed for pedagogical reasons.

What one really was trying to do was to control overtaxing the teachers. Be this pedagogical or not, for the parents this was a regulation that affected their domestic life and that must not be changed unilaterally. By the way, the pedagogical authority ends at the borders of the school property, unless otherwise agreed to previously. Even a pedagogical request – e.g. no television after 8:00 PM – that was not made a condition when the pupil was accepted, cannot be imposed at a later date.

I can hear a chorus of furious teachers exclaim: "Nobody can work like that; this is pure legalistic nonsense!" I can even agree with the latter statement, if it is free of negative connotations. Come to think of it, even with the first one. . . the law is the guardian of the other person. It is a well known human peculiarity that one gladly, if not exclusively, thinks of oneself alone, regardless of whether this involves personal or group egoism. Yet, using the school-free Saturday as an example, it really makes one think about the sentiments of a single mother who takes a course of study on Saturdays, or of one who has, at last, found a job that starts at half past eight o' clock so that she can first take her child to school. She may be the one who exclaims: "Nobody can work like this!" if school is moved up to half past eight. Of course, the school would have good reasons to make a change. But why should the concerns of the school outrank the concerns of the parents?

I have the impression that many of these conflicts could be brought before a judge – in the end, this is what makes a law out of a contract. Regulations without legal recourse are dictatorship. It is not that I find legal proceedings desirable, quite the contrary, yet their availability may prevent certain excesses.

2. External limits are imposed on the freedom given to the teacher by the life of the spirit. In fact, these are twofold. In the first place there are laws and regulations with legal force which apply to both the school and the parents. We need not spend much time to talk about them. A teacher

might think it to be the highest pedagogical wisdom to tear out a pupil's tongue for a lie, yet society protects the child with its penal code. Every citizen knows the way to the prosecutor, the school inspector, the civil judge. This is an area where conflicts are rare. If a teacher should, against all odds, slap a child in the face or become rough, one would consider this a misdemeanor, not a pedagogical liberty.

Cases where the school collides with its own statutes are more interesting. Since parents were justified in assuming that the school abides by its own statutes, they and others can make use of the legal establishment in such cases as well. A special body of advocates could be very helpful here (see chapter 3), because the civil judge is beyond his expertise, if he reads in the statute that this school bases its activity on Rudolf Steiner's pedagogy, and if he then has to decide whether Anthroposophy is taught in the classroom. Multiple choice questions or programmed instructions belong to this category.

3. Finally, it is possible that in regard to a specific pupil, agreements have been made with the parents which violate the school regulations. Such requests should be discussed and decided during entrance discussions. This could involve all sorts of different issues. Perhaps one asks for different vacation times, because the chief breadwinner must take his or her vacation at a different time, or one is asking for a free Monday morning once a month, because the pupil has to visit his far away father that day. One can also agree that the pupil does not have to stay on in school after lessons, when this coincides with music lessons. All this really goes without saying, but if such items are not nailed down in advance, it is justifiable to think that, in case of a conflict situation that arises for quite different reasons, what goes without saying no longer goes at all.

Finally, let us say that the sphere of rights concerns an individual relationship between parents and school. Anything resembling the formation of groups is, therefore, a foreign body in this area, even if it is required by the authorities. The obligation to form a parents council with the right to engage itself with the laws and regulations of the school must be called an abuse of the law. This is true unless the parents are not forced to send their children to a specific school – e.g. one located in their quarter of town. Such a council would make decisions without the responsibility for their consequences (see chapter 2).

Within present practices the parents have little to do with the economic life of the school. They pay their tuition – a question for the sphere of rights! – and feel that this frees them of the problems of the school. (The teachers feel that way about the problems with the parents. . . .) This is usually different during the time of the school's founding, when it is in its formative stage and sometimes in crisis situations! In such cases parents are being appealed to, the problems are being explained in more or less detail, if financial or material help is needed, and an appeal to their generosity is being made. However, should exciting, sensational matters – heaven forbid – become public knowledge, the mood changes to ice. Soothing noises are being made, and the door to the economic sphere is firmly banged shut.

This should be different in a threefold school. Here an associative life should develop that involves all interested parties in the school. The center of this life is found in the economic organ discussed in chapter 1. Here first place is assigned to the parent body with all their wishes, as far as these concern the school (and not only their child). If this organ functions, the desire to be part of a parent council will lose its essential right to exist. As far as the parents are concerned, the school needs to be affordable. But the financial aspect is by no means the main concern in the economic sphere. The first concern is meeting people's needs and whether, or how, they can be met. The finances have to adjust themselves to this. After all, education is no loaf of bread that is sold over the counter for a fixed price.

In such an economic organ, the parents belong together, and they form a group that is not welcome in the other two organs, because they have a collective interest in the existence of the school. Nobody can have a school specially for their own child. My child can go to that school, only because the other pupils, and hence the other parents, make this possible. The possibility to make a school viable is created by the orchestrated working together of many wishes and needs, in an environment of constant give and take.

A model that does justice to this fact is sketched in chapter 7. Parents administer the entire apparatus, including finances, and are in conversation with the teachers. The latter are ready to give the school its (pedagogical) content. However utopian this may sound today, it could become reality more quickly than any of us may anticipate. If the stranglehold of the state increases – and particularly on the schools' curriculum – the Waldorf schools will face the dilemma of choosing between the above sketched structure and slavery. Funding by the state appears to me to be the greatest obstacle against structuring a school in a way that makes it conform to economic reality. Funds flowing to the school as conditional subsidies, have first been taken from the parents and donors in the form of taxes. Now it enables the school to form itself independently from the parents. I consider this just as dangerous as is the direct intervention of the state into freedom in education. A school which is independent of the consumer can afford any whim it chooses.

However much one disagrees, there is another way, and I would like to point to an example. The parents of a therapeutic-pedagogical day school – the Karl König School in Nürnberg – wanted to have a village for their future grown-up disabled people. In close collaboration with the teachers, they refused the subsidies to which they were entitled and which were offered. They undertook the responsibility for financing the project, and in an unparalleled effort, they raised the needed amounts. This made it possible to build up the village in very close collaboration with its future staff, because the model for the life in the village was indeed the Anthroposophical image of man.

The economic cooperation of the parents with the teachers should be carried on both sides by an economic consciousness. Let us refer to a daily occurrence. I can suggest to my greengrocer that he sell bio-dynamic vegetables (as well). If he does not do this, I will not start a quarrel with him. Now I face a common dilemma for a consumer. I have the choice of either making do with his chemically sprayed goods or of shopping at the other end of town, or – third choice – of getting together with others who share my interest and working with them to establish a shop for bio-dynamic goods in our own quarter. However, the comparison does not quite fit. It would be cynical to present the third possibility to the parents. After all, we know that establishing a non-state supported school is nearly impossible, unless one wants to have an accredited Waldorf school. And our hypothetical parents don't want this type of school. Yet, it is well to point out to them that the intractability of their problem is not due to the rigid attitude of the school, but to the state. It is also important to take this forced position of the parents into consideration and to be more forthcoming toward them than would otherwise be necessary.

I have tried to sketch three areas of contact between parents and schools: the life of the spirit, human rights, and the economic life. The nature of the encounter turned out to be different in each case. We did not discuss the many groups of parents that form around young schools and take over the task of the latter. Such groups would achieve their functional significance only in an alternative school, administered by the parents. Today they are in a somewhat tragic situation. Either they are delegations that lack the autonomy of a republican mandate whereby the school decides that certain activities may be performed by parents and it can intervene at any time, terminate the activities, etc. which it often does as soon as the tasks can be taken over by it own employees. In this case the parents feel expelled. Or, real indigenous alternatives are chosen. These then take place more or less outside the school, for instance, conducting a bazaar, the yield of which goes to the school. However positively these methods of self-help may be judged, never will they replace the conversations between school, teachers, and parents. The courage to conduct these conversations needs to be found.

Chapter 6

The Waldorf School and State Funding

A Waldorf school has three sources of income: the tuition fees coming from the parents, the free gifts from various private people and organizations, and the moneys placed at the disposal of the schools by their state or country. One could add a fourth one, namely the teachers who, in order to make this pedagogy a reality in the world, make do with lesser remuneration compared to similar efforts in other schools.

The Waldorf school is designed to be financed by free gifts. The principal sources Steiner had in mind are industrial surpluses. These are funds donated by individual enterprises, clearly donations, by today's laws, yet from a macro-social point of view, these represent compensations paid by the totality of the economy to the totality of the spiritual life. Parental tuition payments are for the most part payments for effort. How many parents continue to pay tuition after their offspring has left the school? By the nature of the pedagogic effort, they are forced to pay not only for their children's lessons, but also for the whole institution, including the training of the teachers. It is consequently logical that they, in turn, place demands on the school. In state supported schools these demands step quite openly into the foreground. Conditions that clash with the principles of the Waldorf school occur so often that parents do not know which way to turn to get state support without betraying their goal.[5]

State support is an evil from the point of view of the threefold order. I say this in the face of the idea that the state redistributes what was first taken from the parents by way of taxes, and that consequently the school – and through the school, the parents – only get what they are entitled to. From a macro-social point of view, this is certainly correct, but on the institutional level it does not remove the evil influence created by this redistribution. I would even make the dictum that state support never supports, i.e. it hurts the school more than it helps. One could allow the state to play the role of accountant, only if a public law would entitle the pupil to an educational voucher, which would give him or her access to any desired school, of course only if the school will admit him or her.

I certainly do not wish to say that one should refuse state support under all circumstances. Alternatives should be weighed against each other in each individual case. It may require as much courage to accept state support as to be "bad with the bad ones." I have seldom heard anything about such deliberations. I have the impression that one longs for state support, which is quite understandable from certain perspectives! One is ready from the start to trade one's right of the first born against a handful of silver. Sometimes it is quite wel-

---

[5] By the way, the above often applies equally to schools without state support in a number of states. This regal right is being curtailed to a greater or lesser degree in different places. Strasburg made Great Britain (and thus all states under British jurisdiction) put a stop to it. In the Netherlands the highest court ruled (based on their charter of freedom?) that no legal requirement for going to school can stop parents, who are dissatisfied with the existing schools from educating their children themselves.

come, if the state guards the school from difficult alternatives with its statutes.

In the Netherlands, state support is granted only if one is establishing an association, a foundation, or a church school, or, of course, a state school. This excludes an entrepreneur who runs his own private school at his own risk. Dear state, thanks a lot for your regulations! If one is a foundation or association, one acquires a board of directors, and the staff become employees. This guarantees discipline, and everyone can have access to unemployment compensation. Dear state, thanks a lot for your regulations! The state accepts the teacher training for Waldorf schools, at least for its own system. This gives the "Bund" a monopoly for teacher training. Basically, this forces the school to join the collaboration and leads to the possibility of determining the conduct of the schools and seminars by way of the joint association of schools. Peace reigns in the house. Thanks a lot, dear state! One could plod along for a bit longer in this fashion.

"It cannot be done without state support." This statement can be heard everywhere, but this statement needs to be challenged. To be sure, if debt financing is used to build the school, one sits pretty with support. And if the staff is used to upper class wages, it is true as well. That's why it is so hard to switch over. But short-circuiting the problem, by saying that the parents cannot afford to pay the subsidies, does not get one anywhere.

Even though it does not apply to a school but to a therapeutic home, I would like to cite the following example. It took place many years ago, and the numbers may have to be trebled for our time, but we are not talking about inflation. In this home one calculated the daily cost of a bed at $9.57. I visited there several times and know that it certainly was not a shabby place. Both the physical and emotional care were exceptional. One unfortunate day, the possibility of state support materialized. It was impossible to resist the temptation, and within half a year the daily cost per bed went up to $45.24 – almost five times as much as before. Within two years the state-supported unnecessary extras were considered to be essential necessities by those who lived there. One felt it to be impossible to go on working without those things.

Of course, I am not trying to say that the running costs of the Waldorf schools would be reduced to one fifth. Yet again, it is also wrong to look at the deficit due to lack of state support as a given entity that has to be made good by the parents. The experience of the few schools in Germany which are not state supported and of the very large, similarly independent schools in England tells a different tale. The school in Wernstein even managed with parental contributions alone. The school asked for free donations and based this on the idea that, if the parents really wanted the school they would also see to it that the teachers earned a living. Because the parents could take their children out of the school at any time, one had to live up to one's standards from day to day. Here, too, we may say because death was built in, the school lived.[6] I am not saying that one can manage without state support or even without tuition. I merely state that the conditions for running a truly free Waldorf school have as yet hardly been investigated.

To say that state support and the threefold order are incompatible would be an exaggeration. The functioning of the Waldorf school in Pforzheim and that of the threefold

---

[6] I want to add this brief note, because the history of the Wernstein school is well known, and someone could counter my statement by saying that Wernstein, too, had asked for state support. Wernstein had nine or ten grades and no intention to go beyond this. The state, however, forced one to do that. The reason was that, in accordance with the law of compulsory education, Wernstein could be considered a school only as a Waldorf school. The federation ("Bund") of Waldorf schools had registered the school as preparatolry for the matriculation exam - again probably with state support in mind. According to the state, if Wernstein had continued not to prepare for matriculation, it would cease to be a Waldorf school and have had to close its doors. The specific local situation made financing the remaining higher grade unaffordable, thus forcing Wernstein under the yoke of state support.

school in Amsterdam (at that time) are proof to the contrary. One can, however, state that where schools have to manage without state support, a threefold structure is automatically being attempted. Wernstein is one example: another one is a school for children with learning disorders in Bergen. However, if one fails to be conscious of the daily influence of state support, the life in a school gets rapidly perverted, i.e. one starts to call something healthy, when it is really sick.

This is why one should not accept state support as a matter of course. One could turn it into a sacramental act: not a prayer of thanks but an oath to their own conscience on the part of every staff member. There must be a holy oath given by every individual to his or her colleagues and a solemn oath on the part of the school: "Every condition for support that damages Rudolf Steiner's goal for the institution is to be rejected, even if it means bankruptcy!" This is what would happen vis-à-vis a private donor as a matter-of-course. Every member of the staff should have free access to the board of advocates, so as to prevent enlarged consciences in case of emergencies. This could be reinforced by having the courage to engage in a legal battle, even if the case may seem hopeless, even if the relationship with the authorities is clouded. One should involve every legal level all the way to the constitutional judge, all the way to Washington, D.C., if only to gain publicity. It would be well to create a strike fund, financed by the entire international Waldorf school movement. This would defray the legal costs and, additionally, assure the survival of the school, at least until the battle all the way up to the highest court has been decided. If all else fails, a march of 500 to 800 pupils to the U.S. Department of Education should be considered. This would give the people behind their desks, who know all about how children should be brought up, the opportunity to translate their knowledge into action.

I know the argument: don't use the children as a weapon. I agree. Yet why shouldn't the ones who are really involved demonstrate that not the teachers but the pupils bear the wounds of ideological ostrich behavior, bureaucratic arrogance, and economic interests?

Chapter 7

An Alternate Threefold Structure

Schools often start with the parents. *They* look for a Waldorf school for their children, and *they* act to find teachers, a building, and money. *They* are the ones who discuss the development with the teachers. Later on, they are often in for a great disappointment when they are – suddenly or gradually – forced out of the school. Is this really necessary? Certainly not.

True, one cannot imagine a Waldorf school where parents discuss the methods of teaching with the teachers. The teachers have the prerogative of administering the details of the pedagogical process. There is, however, no reason why those parents on a path of anthroposophy cannot make the school viable. Why can they not take over the administration or the running of the school? Perhaps, as administrators, they can negotiate the pay and conditions under which the teachers do their jobs. They may themselves even choose the teachers. This would result in a structure governed by economical considerations, namely from the point of view that nothing can be produced without a need for it, "not even truth." (Rudolf Steiner, GA 190)

I will not fill in this picture with more detail, simply because, to my knowledge, no such Waldorf schools exist. Thus one has no recourse to experience, so a description remains a somewhat unrealistic theory. Yet to provide a feeling that this is nothing obtuse, I might mention that at least two therapeutic institutions work on this basis in the Netherlands. The healthcare workers (including the doctors) negotiate the amount they need to accomplish their work with the patients – who also administer the undertaking. The ***Training for Threefoldness*** (Ausbilding für Dreigliederung) is based on this principle and even closer to a Waldorf school. I will simply describe how this undertaking is structured. (See also my ***Training for Threefoldness*** in the Netherlands, ***Info 3***, 1988/6.)

The training takes two years, and each course stands on its own. Continuity is not to be assumed. When the first people who wished training in threefoldness came along, they were told that, if they wanted such training, they had to take care of the following: students, docents, rooms, a place, schedules and desired content of the training, the latter to be discussed with docents, based on what was desired in connection with what was needed. Finally, they had to determine the honorarium for which the docents would be willing to provide the content of the course. By the way, it turned out that every other year the students tried, without being asked, to provide a starting point for the next group. Biannually, it thus depends on the initiative of the students whether or not the training continues. In the course of events, it was discovered that no absolute freedom existed in the choice of docents. The interaction of the group was as much a unit by itself as was the content of the course. Inversely, it was found that wishes for content that were noted by the docent with some skepticism were fully justified. As to the financial side? This was far simpler than anticipated.

I'll stop with these mere indications. They may suffice to show that institutions, created on a need base, are absolutely viable. However, they require a pronounced flexibility. I would count this as a plus.

Chapter 8

A School with Two Classes of Faculty?

On several occasions we had to point to the tendency to differentiate between two classes of faculty members in a Waldorf school, the higher and the lower level ones. I had intended to treat this subject with a footnote, but it is really more important than that.

In a certain sense, there have always been two classes in society, the have and the have-nots. Yet the more we go back in history we find that this, doubtless real, duality was felt much more as personal destiny, particularly so in pre-Christian days. The division into three, and sometimes even more, estates played a greater role in society than wealth. The original system of castes went through several reincarnations, such as the three estates of the Middle Ages. In our time a system of six classes (really three with each one having an upper and a lower level) has been developed in the United States in the thirties of our century, a quite informal phenomenon, yet one that defines a person's whole life. Today's system of two classes (Aristocrats and Proletarians) is modeled more on the Roman model. It continues throughout the Middle Ages as Fathers versus Brothers (Patres contra Fratres). Today it surfaces in a new version, in what we call the Social Entitlement or Welfare State. The majority of the population is divided into those who live off their own work and those who depend on public support. The ideological background of this arrangement is that one does not leave the unemployed to starve (as one had done in England starting in the eighteenth century and in all the western world in the nineteenth century), but keeps them alive with minimal public support. In this way a wedge is driven into the proletariat (the Welfare State was an invention of the Christian parties), and a reserve of willing workers is created. One manipulates the difference in the income of the workers and the unemployed, so that the worker is in constant fear of losing his job, and the unemployed will take every opportunity to rise up to the level of the higher standard of life of the employed. (The fact that oddballs exist who are totally uninterested in these distinctions is of as little importance as is the existence of people who live off their capital.)

This tendency toward polarization can be found in Waldorf schools as well. I am not talking about the observation I made every day as a pupil, that the majority of the teachers go to the teachers room during breaks, and a smaller number gather at the janitor's. It is sad, and only too human, but these two groups were simply mad at each other on an ideological basis. We are talking about a consciously created bipartisanship that can occur in any number of endeavors.

For example, schools offer parents workshops on the anthroposophical view of mankind, not so much because the parents have this interest, or at least this is not the main reason. (other arrangements are available for this.) One really does it to create a set of friends who carry the school, who can be entrusted with tasks, and from whose ranks one can perhaps choose functionaries, members of the executive board, class parents, members of the parental council, representatives of the parents in discussions with officialdom, etc. Socially, this sort of thing has a destructive effect. It divides the parents into two groups: those who carry responsibility, and those who are not assigned responsibilities. The latter continually collide with a closed front of teachers and responsible parents. These either develop the well known aggressive attitude, complete with conspiracies or – depending on inclination – toadyism to get on the right side.

In some schools there is a similar division between the teachers who carry responsibility and the colleagues who cannot be entrusted with such responsibilities. A judgment is being pronounced wherever belonging to an inner circle is treated as a special qualification, i.e. as being superior to the remaining colleagues, and the social basis of the school is being undermined. Does not one have to expect that someone who feels excluded, who feels himself as a lesser person will then start to try to prove that the chosen ones – perhaps morally – are inferior?

I have mentioned the esoteric circle. In this connection I have stressed that this must remain a purely spiritual matter, i.e. that nothing must *directly* become part of the way the school is managed. Most of those who are interested in Waldorf schools probably already know that teachers who so desire (in other words who are being admitted) already have an esoteric connection. Of course, there is nothing wrong with this, not even exclusivity. This is part of human freedom. It merely must remain in the purely spiritual sphere. The matter assumes a black aspect and has socially decomposing effects as soon as it becomes a brotherhood, and as soon as one has to belong to a certain circle for specific functions.

In summary, I would like to say that it is possible to form exclusive circles. In that case, one must be careful that what happens in such circles is fenced off from the routine of the school. In principle, such a circle should be open to every colleague, although one is at liberty to demand specific capabilities for specific areas of work. One will hardly invite the lady who cleans the classrooms to participate in new legislation. A school with two classes of workers is a relapse into a pre-Christian formation. Just like a political two-class society, it remains a power structure in its own area, embellish it as you will.

AWSNA Publications

Appendix A

Had Rudolf Steiner not blessed the marriage between the Waldorf school movement and the Threefold Social Order, it would probably never have come about. The Waldorf school is the child of the Threefold Social Order. As a small piece of free spiritual life, it is what remains of the wreck of the Threefold Social Order. In the future it will give birth to a new Threefold Order. In the meantime, many leaders of the Waldorf school movement feel obligated to present the activities and omissions of this movement as the realization of the Threefold Order. Of course, this results in a quarrel. This quarrel has really been raging for a long time and is masked by the fact that the pedagogical leaders are posing as experts in Threefoldness. As long as the true proponents of the Threefold Order are asleep or silenced, others are more or less free to define what threefoldness is. On top of this, it is easy for them to do this, because the majority of Anthroposophists, including the Waldorf teachers, have hardly an inkling of the Threefold Social Order.

(The original German then goes on to dissect the Constitution of the Bund der Freie Waldorfschulen in Germany. The editor feels this is not relevant for English readers and has deleted it.)

AWSNA Publications

Appendix B

A Micro-Social Excursion

It is really only too understandable, if all that stems from the social impulse encounters discomfort. True, the church has for centuries used "caritas", i.e. doing good works towards those in need, as an educational tool. But even the church basically retained the self as focus, because benevolence was propagated as the key to heaven for the soul. The bourgeoisie further perverted it by placing demands and conditions on being worthy of help, for example through church attendance. Relatively small groups (like the original Franciscans or the Chassidim), or individual persons (like some of the saints), really acted based on the misery of the other person, which is to say they made material sacrifices not, as it were, as the price for the salvation of their own soul. On the institutional level, the social impulse had practically no impact at all. At that level we have lived in a social decline for nearly the last two thousand years. The consciousness of the group – subordinating one's own interests to that of the group which was the former carrier of the social impulse – has been replaced by a consciousness aimed at the advantage of the individual (basic sociological law). One should not be surprised that everything based on the social impulse is being felt as being unrealistic, if not obtuse, or even insane. Indeed, the social impulse turns every human and institutional habit upside down.

The fact that the social impulse as a matter of Christianity is still in its early infancy is no reason to make a wide circle around this painful subject. I want to conclude by shedding light from this impulse on a part of our everyday life. We have already pointed out that the other person is taboo from the point of view of the social life. It is not up to me to judge his peculiarities, his demeanor, his (non-)manners, in short, his entire being as he is. The moment I correct the other, he has become an object. In this case I deny him his basic equality with myself. It is not merely a matter of "telling so-and-so the truth for a change", nor the veiled reprimand, "Why on earth do you do it in this way?" – or, whatever form one chooses to give one's disapproval. In all these instances, one wishes to have the other be different from the way he is. What gives us the right to do this?

This understanding does not in itself achieve anything of a social nature; it remains within the life of the spirit. What is social lives exclusively in deeds, even if they are the non-actions of restraint. I may recognize that the other person has exactly the same right to his idiosyncrasy as do I, even if this appears to me as inept. This recognition is only the precondition for the creation of something of a social nature, namely to make the need of someone else the motive of my action. If I still find that his need requires a correction on his part, I merely do away with my problems with him.

One cannot and should not require of anyone to respect the essence of the other person. One can merely try to do it oneself in total freedom. In this way, it may possibly happen in the long run that one takes the other the way he is, not merely because one understands this, but because it has become a matter of course in one's soul. These are steps on the ascent to the social human being. In the meantime, one can stop oneself from bothering others with one's judgment. As we shall see, one can even prohibit such judgmental utterances in connection with the social life, because they deal with external matters. "No dark sinister court has named you as a judge," says Christian Morgenstern in one of his poems. There is only one exception to this: when the other person asks me for a judgment. In this case I am allowed to give it, not because I want to change him, but because he himself wishes to change.

This gives an approximate picture of what one could call the "Uriel gesture",[7] in fact the fundamental social atmosphere. We shall see that institutional life requires an additional framework of conditions, but let us stay in the microsphere for a while longer. The first problem we encounter here is whether a question has been asked and, if this is the case, whether it is directed at me. "I wish somebody would make me give up smoking!" This can be rhetoric, can be directed toward the search for the right helper, and could also be a call for help in my direction. If one is not sure that it is indeed the latter, it is best to be silent. The question not asked is a similar case. Not everyone is able to call for help. But many consider themselves to be so clairvoyant that they hear calls for help that do not exist. Here, too, the social impulse bids us be silent if we are not quite sure of ourselves – even if only to give the person in need time to better articulate his call for help.

Such reticence is unfashionable. In the past it arose from a group consciousness as custom and etiquette. Typically, it did not apply toward someone from a "lower estate." It should have become part of the "I", is not recognized as a positive reality, but transformed into its opposite. It must be possible to "discuss" everything, meaning that one can tell another to his face all that one thinks about him. The psychologists tell us that this reduces tensions. Large amounts are being paid for professionally conducted swear sessions. This is not even anything new. The Tibetans have long known about the emptying of the soul and its effect on one's feeling of well-being. Once a year, everyone is allowed to scream at everyone with whatever one has against him. In contrast, this

---

[7] Uriel, the least known of the four archangels. See Chronicles I, 6:24 and 15:5-11, also Rudolf Steiner in GA 229 (1955) IV. In the middle ages Uriel was known under his Greek name Orphiel as a spirit of Saturn. See Rudolf Steiner in GA 265 (1987) 336.

was strictly forbidden on any other day. And on that particular day one was wise enough to . . . plug up one's ears.

It is simply not true that talk which disqualifies the other person solves any problem, except perhaps the one of how one can get rid of one's indignation. "This clears the air," takes place at the expense of the other person. Nobody, except saints, can stand criticism of his sense of self. There are people capable of disguising or idealizing the fact that they are offended. The feeling is most often unconscious, but nevertheless very real, but when one is being criticized, one has the experience of not having been dealt with as a person but as an object that can be changed like a tool that does not quite fit the hand. Steiner calls this sort of criticism the modern form of torture. The dialogue, according to Goethe: "more refreshing than light" is being abused for black magic. Take the wondrous, so-called therapeutic dialogue as an example. Used for healing, it takes its departure from everyone's effort to search how much guilt he has regarding certain difficulties. This is transformed into its black magical counter when those present look for a scapegoat who gets all the blame.

Personally, I refuse to accept unasked for criticism of my own person. If someone finds it necessary to look for an inner deformation behind my interpretation – be it the assumption that I got out of bed with the wrong foot, or the statement that I am unfit due to certain inner deficiencies in order to . . . , the discussion is terminated. By the way, the reasons for this are not merely social theory and so-called social hygiene, but practical reasons as well. Such a discussion almost always ends in quarrels and hate.

> I shot an arrow in the air
> It fell to earth, I knew not where;
>
> Long, long afterward, in an oak
> I found the arrow, still unbroke
>
> – Longfellow, 1845

Well, should one then swallow everything? Before we approach this question, let me say that the consequences of a personal criticism uttered in indignation, anger, or rage are as a rule less catastrophic than carefully prepared advice and exhortations. After all, one knows from one's own experience that in the heat of passion, one is often driven to utterances which one did not mean the way they came out. In this situation the element of being treated as an object is nowhere as strongly experienced. Swear words are relatively harmless. It is my experience that so-called therapeutic and pedagogical comments hurt far more. These hurt even if they are disguised as a criticism of the subject on hand. Deep down, the censured person can tell very well whether the criticism is personal or directed at the problem.

Having said this, let us observe that in this respect, too, convention is stood on its head, if we want to do justice to the social impulse. Just as one can defend oneself when one is the object of exhortation, one can take the initiative when one is tempted to play the instructor, not, of course, by pointing out his imperfect behavior to one's protagonist, but by asking him to be mindful of one's own weakness. "Here we have another nicotine addict who poisons the air," leads, if not to a break, at least to resentment. "Would you be willing not to smoke in this room, because the smoke does not agree with me?" This makes the cause of the contrasting interests my weakness and my inability to change (even if, and particularly when, there is a physiological reason for this).

I would be misunderstood, if one were to see a moral teaching in the above. I am talking about the real interface between human beings, something we prefer to be blind to. And it flatters our self-image, if we can clothe our vice in the cloak of helpfulness. In case of conflicts, we prefer to see the splinter in the other person's eye rather than the beam in our own; let him change. Even the thought that one could change oneself seldom surfaces. There we have our normal attitude simply carried to extremes; we want to change the other person like an object that annoys us. Our self-created technocracy is based on wanting to make the human being function within society. But, where the other person's behavior gets to be unbearable and where the request to consider our own weakness does not help, negative judgment won't help either. In this case one can take recourse to the judge as last neutral resort. He hands out what we have a right to by law – and we are not entitled to anything more.

This says that the above problem: a question of the law – "law" taken in the widest sense, the "I" and "you." If we enter into another sphere, the gesture of Uriel is valid only within limits. Let us briefly discuss this, so as to avoid mix-ups and misunderstandings.

Within the sphere of the spiritual life, i.e. the relationship of the soul to the spiritual world, the question does not concern the other person; it concerns the truth. Here a (spiritual) battle reigns, i.e. competition. The freedom of the person of a different opinion to express it is countered by mine to fight the very root of that opinion. Here there exists neither a right nor a duty to take it easy as long as one scrupulously observes what the other person has publicly stated. Whoever has considered his output ripe for the public must expose it to the latter's criticism. Inversely, it is proper that one ignores what was not meant for publication. This is true of what one knows from personal discussions as much as from unpublished lectures of Rudolf Steiner, the former perhaps more for social reasons, the latter more for reasons of social hygiene. This applies to the dead as well – counter to modern fashion.

Reasons and motives which have led someone to statements or deeds also belong to what is not meant for publicity. Often the other person will himself have the urge to proclaim his reasons. Unless he does, hypotheses and imputations show a lack of respect for the other's life of the soul. "From a certain point of view, it is even simply a violation of the personality to search for deeper causes of a decision." The inquiry, "How did you get to this conclusion?" is permissible only as long as the spiritual life remains in the realm of thinking. After all, thought can be retraced. "He has had poor experiences with Dornach; that's why he is against networking the Threefold Order." Such a statement primarily leads away from the point of contention and is more generally unhygienic socially. It is quite beside the point that the hypothesis is incorrect. Most imputations express a qualification, either a positive or a negative one. They belong to the area of the life of rights, even if they are not forbidden, specifically to the area of the "inner right."

Mr. Correct is at liberty to get excited, because I have forgotten a comma, or because my presentations of the Threefold Order may be totally wrong, even if his choice of words is inappropriate to the importance of the subject. We remain within the spiritual sphere. But if he ascribes a forgotten comma to my difficulties with punctuation and these in turn perhaps to a deformation of the soul, he trespasses into an area that is none of his business and makes no progress in solving the problem. One can only reject this in the sharpest terms. If he calls my ideas regarding the Threefold Order pure Communism, one can argue about it. But if he calls me a Communist, he has lost the respect we all observe vis-à-vis the other person and should not be surprised to get a slap in the face – of course, spoken figuratively.

There are exceptions. Anyone who consciously publishes untruths – something one is rarely able to know – deserves no protection. Having uncovered his method, one has a right to state that it is not worthwhile to take it seriously and paying further attention to his elaboration is a waste of time, because he has eliminated himself as partner in the discussion. Again, this must be done without making him personally lose face.

Again, it needs to be said that the social hygiene we are talking about is far from a matter of course. The rather superfluous surface varnish of fair treatment displayed toward the output of an author only too often has a background of personal suspicions.

After airing these basic considerations, derived directly from the social impulse, the question arises of how these problems shape up in the meso-sphere. Particularly within the institutional life, i.e. wherever people work together toward a common goal, personal judgments, from innuendoes to condemnations, are pure poison. Yet the very working together toward a goal may make it necessary to correct what the colleague does. Does the social impulse leave us in the lurch in this dilemma?

First, we need to state that we invariably find a life of the spirit, a life of rights, and an economic life in every institution, to whatever part of society it may belong. In the micro-life where we deal with others, the differentiation is left to the discretion of the individual. Due to its own life of rights, the institution is in a position to structure behavior in the three spheres. For example, the fact that within the life of the spirit all criticism that serves the search for truth (in non personal areas) is allowed, does not mean that it may be aired at any time and place. After all, the institution works toward a specific goal, and this may demand certain constraints. Yet the institution must never block this airing of any position whatever, regardless of time and place. On the other side of the coin is the institution's economic life, which represents the efficiency of the organization. This demands a structure of command and correction within certain limits, which I won't discuss here. Where would we be if the foreman could not correct and decide? It will seldom be taken wrongly if rough words are used, because the work at hand and the situation explain this. "Would you please," will hardly be considered an insult. In contrast, the drill sergeant swears at the recruit: "Can you go even slower, you donkey!" The recruit immediately feels the intention to put him down.

The way in which criticism can take place in an institution finds its hygienic expression in the democratic-republican principle (see chapter 2.) Here I merely want to deal with two aspects that touch directly on our theme: The first one is the area of tasks to be accomplished. Here mandates are assigned democratically. During their time of validity, any type of criticism of the way the carrier of a mandate carries it out is forbidden, even in the form of "questions" and "suggestions." Only in emergency cases can the mandate be prematurely terminated, but the carrier of the mandate cannot be criticized even then. Although this principle goes back to Steiner, it has to be said that it is not even commonly adhered to by Anthroposophical institutions. The way the other person does his job is only too often subject to "signals" or other euphemistically circumscribed fault finding. Only when the carrier of a mandate can be sure that his work is not being foul-mouthed, can he feel free to ask colleagues for advice and, perhaps, look for the cause for not so happy results in his own activities. Only then does the institution truly commence to breathe. The second aspect involves the actual areas of rights of an institution: the prohibitions and, at times, the commands as well. These are democratically created and confront the staff with the fact that what they can mentally accept, they cannot always realize in life (reality). One can see (mental) that one should not arrive at work too late – and still get up too late (reality). One can accept that one should not get too close to the pretty sex – and still allow one's fingers to wander.

It is unacceptable to allow everybody to play the moralist in this area. Such a practice would introduce the poison of personal criticism into the life of the institution, should there be violations against democratic decisions. We have learned to know such criticism to be anti-social. How can one escape this dilemma? The answer is the supervisor. This person is democratically elected, based on the recognition that adherence to the agreement needs to be controlled and, if need be, enforced. This person, too, refrains from moralizing. This unpleasant office is to be rotated rapidly. He alerts the "offender" to the fact that his action went against the rules. If this does not help, he will communicate the observation to the organ of rights. Here, too, no moralizing takes place. "How can it be that an educated person like yourself can again

. . . ." is degrading. The rights organ will do no more than state the consequences of the unruly behavior.

To be sure, it is impossible to carefully regulate every conceivable thing that might occur. Certainly one can forbid rudeness, noxious to the goal of the institution, but one cannot command courtesy. "Don't always slam the door in front of my nose!" is something one can hardly prohibit, neither the rude slamming of the door, nor the rude remark. On the other hand, one will permit only the chairperson to interrupt the speaker in a meeting. By his function he is uninvolved. Not, "Don't interrupt me again!" but: "Dear Chairperson, will you please see to it that I will not be interrupted!"

I must say it again: unfortunately it is customary in many institutions to do exactly the opposite. One hates to forbid anything. "Such things have to evolve in the dynamic process of working together." Instead, all sorts of people who feel qualified to do this "enlighten the conscience" of those working in the institution. In the end the latter acquires the smell of moral acidity and those who work there the smell of worse. Now the psychologists enter and get going on conditioning and motivation with psycho technical know-how. This can certainly help for the moment. But one has to recognize that this help grows out of the therapeutic instead of the social impulse, and that the result can, therefore, not be a social one. One can even predict this without examples. Treating the human being as an object has to come to the surface. This has to be prevented from the start by excluding the personality of the individual from any debate. "The dignity of the human being is not to be touched." Taken seriously, this sentence of the constitution exactly describes the gesture of Uriel.